Zeal with KNOWLEDGE
The First Sixty Years of FEAST / APTS

WILLIAM W. MENZIES
JOHN F. CARTER
DAVE JOHNSON

New Expanded Edition
WIPF & STOCK · Eugene, Oregon

Wipf and Stock Publishers
199 W 8th Ave, Suite 3
Eugene, OR 97401

Zeal with Knowledge
The First Sixty Years of FEAST/APTS - New Expanded Edition
By Menzies, William W. and Carter, John F.
Copyright © 2024 Asia Pacific Theological Seminary Press (APTS Press) All rights reserved.
Softcover ISBN-13: 979-8-3852-1590-4
Hardcover ISBN-13: 979-8-3852-1591-1
eBook ISBN-13: 979-8-3852-1592-8
Publication date 2/9/2024
Previously published by Asia Pacific Theological Seminary Press (APTS Press), 2024

to the Second Edition

This revised edition is lovingly dedicated to all who have served at FEAST/APTS at any time, long or short, or part time, at any point in the journey. Your contribution is a part of this story, for the glory of God alone.

Preface

As the twentieth century was drawing to a close and the administration and faculty of APTS began to anticipate the challenges and opportunities to be encountered in twenty-first century, I asked Dr. William Menzies, noted Assemblies of God theologian, historian and former APTS president, to initiate the writing of a history of the first forty years of FEAST/APTS. Knowing that Dr. Menzies had collected materials and resources for this purpose for a number of years and had, himself, been deeply involved in the school since the 1980s, it was obvious that he was uniquely qualified for this task. This seemed an especially appropriate time for such an undertaking since all of the former FEAST/APTS presidents were still available to give input and the scheduling of the 40th anniversary celebration in March 2004 provided a suitable occasion for its release. Furthermore, it seemed fitting to document how God had led missions and national leaders over four decades to develop and maintain a school such as APTS.

Dr. Menzies completed an initial draft by early 2001. Building on his substantial work, additional material and detail were added covering primarily the years since I assumed the APTS presidency in 1996. The former presidents and others who played a significant role in the school were also asked to review initial drafts to ensure completeness and accuracy.

Much of this history comes from the first-person accounts of those who were directly involved, especially those who served in the role of president. In addition to these reflections, catalogs, school annuals, board minutes, presidential reports, internal memoranda, photo collections and other documents were consulted. Since few of these are public documents and the content was verified by those directly involved, we determined that it would be of limited value to footnote such sources. However, all sources remain a part of the APTS archives and are available to anyone interested in further research.

The FEAST/APTS story provides a striking example of God's sovereign direction of missionaries, educators and national leaders over many years to develop an institution of exceptional quality for training of young men and women for Pentecostal ministry in their own nations. As a fundamental strategy to advance the kingdom of God around the world, the training of national leaders has remained a significant emphasis of Assemblies of God missions to this day. I pray that this accounting of the events that led to the development of FEAST/APTS will serve as an inspiration to those who continue to devote themselves to the Great Commission ministry.

John F. Carter, Ph.D.
Baguio City, Philippines
February 2004

Preface
to the Second Edition

When the APTS leadership decided to update the history of APTS, I was honored when President Yee asked me to write the updated part of the story. By this time, one of the co-authors, Dr. William Menzies, had gone on to his eternal reward and the other, Dr. John Carter, had fully retired.

While any writer's style is always somewhat different than others, I have tried to follow the same themes and emphasis as the original edition, making it as reasonably seamless as possible. That being said, this book is not an exhaustive history of APTS and makes no claim to be. Nor do we even attempt to measure the incredible impact that APTS has made on the Asia Pacific, Northern Asia and Pacific Oceana parts of the world, which is also part of our remit. Because this account is being produced as part of the 60th anniversary celebration of APTS and intended to be celebratory in nature, no objectivity is claimed.

Much of the research was done with archival materials such as minutes of meetings, accreditation studies and the like. I have also solicited viewpoints from long-time faculty members who were here during the period and anyone else that might have insights or memories of what has happened over the last twenty years. I am thankful to the publishers for allowing me to use portions of my previous publications, *Led by The Spirit: The History of the American Assemblies of God Missionaries in the Philippines* (Pasig City, Philippines: ICI Ministries, Inc., 2009) and "FEAST/APTS in Historical Retrospect," Parts I and II, in the *Asian Journal of Pentecostal Studies* (Vol. 17.1 February, 2014).

John Carter, as a co-author of the first edition, also reviewed this part of the manuscript and gave his input.

Photo selection proved to be difficult. Every effort was made to provide a variety of pictures that help tell the story of APTS through the years. Unfortunately, a number of pictures from the first edition either no longer survive in digital format or had to be discarded in order to keep the number of pictures reasonable once the photos from the new edition were added. To any whose picture is not included for any reason and should have been, the APTS Press leadership offers their humblest apologies.

The mission of APTS to train workers under the leadership of the Holy Spirit for the Lord's harvest in Asia and Pacific Oceania remains unchanged, although the methods and strategies to do so must be altered from time to time. This expanded edition includes the story of how this has been done over the last twenty years, taking into account the rapid changes in technology and educational delivery systems, especially in light of the COVID-19 pandemic. I hope you enjoy the story.

Dave Johnson, D.Miss.
Author of the Expanded Chapters

Acknowledgments
for the Second Edition

No one ever writes a book alone and this book is no exception. I would like to extend thanks to the following people. Raciel Kines retyped the original manuscript because the digital files got lost over the ensuring years. Jemon Subang, the registrar, and his staff provided the enrollment data, number of graduates of the GMC programs, the names of the outstanding students of the era and the data on the alumni found in Appendix A. Beverly Conceja, the personal assistant to the academic dean, provided me with a list of faculty and missionaries who have served during this time, as well as the materials in Appendices C and D. Sol Sacbat, the library supervisor, provided the data on the current library holdings. Ely Sebiano, the staff personnel manager, provided Appendix B. Drs. John Carter, Galen Herweck and Tham Wan Yee for reviewing the revised portion of the manuscript. Dr. Carter provided the pictures from the first edition and Dr. Galen Hertweck provided the bulk of the pictures for the years 2004-23. Jemon Subang and his assistant, Mark Jude Butron, helped with the archival materials from the Asia Pacific Research Center on the APTS Baguio City campus. Joanna (Twinkle) Fallorin-Reynaldo and Alpha Magno, the APTS marketing assistants, also helped with the manuscript from time to time and Alpha will be responsible for marketing the book. Debbie Johnson, Larry Brooks and Mil Santos of the APTS Press editorial team worked hard to prepare the manuscript and Debbie, my wife, put up with me in the research and writing process with all of the thrills and spills that accompany such efforts. To anyone else who may have helped, any errors are entirely my responsibility. And more than anything, my profound thanks to Jesus Christ, my Lord and Savior, without whom none of this would have any purpose or meaning.

Table of Contents

iii	Dedication
v	Preface
vii	Preface to the Second Edition
ix	Acknowledgments for the Second Edition
1	Introduction
3	The Birth of An Idea
7	Humble Beginnings: (1960-1964)
11	The Early Years: (1965-1972)
17	Years of Consolidation: (1972-1984)
25	From Manila to Baguio City; From FEAST to APTS: (1985-1989)
29	PHOTO GALLERY 1
39	The Decade of Harvest: The 1990s and Early 2000s
67	Into the New Millennium
69	PHOTO GALLERY 2
75	A New Season: (2004-2014)
99	PHOTO GALLERY 3

107	International, Pentecostal, and Missional: (2014-2024)
129	Appendix A
186	Appendix B
189	Appendix C
190	Appendix D

Introduction

Situated one mile above sea level in the Cordillera mountain range on the island of Luzon in northern Philippines, 150 miles (250 km) north of Manila, and commanding a spectacular view of mountains and ravines lies the beautiful campus of Asia Pacific Theological Seminary (APTS). As the flagship graduate theological school for the Assemblies of God of Asia and the vast Pacific Rim, APTS is a dynamic center of spiritual and academic development, serving students from more than twenty nations each year. A highly qualified multi-national missionary faculty, themselves representing a half-dozen or more nationalities, provides a comprehensive and demanding academic program.

Over the forty years of the school's existence, the alumni have gone out to serve in significant roles of leadership in the churches of the Assemblies of God and many other denominations throughout the region. A significant proportion of the administrators and faculty members of the approximately seventy-five Assemblies of God Bible Schools and extension centers in Asia Pacific are alumni of APTS. Pastors of great urban churches and pioneers in remote and difficult places have been trained at APTS. Many national church leaders in their respective Assemblies of God fellowships have received their ministry training at APTS. Increasingly, graduates are moving into foreign missions service, representing Asian national churches that are catching the vision of taking the gospel to the unreached peoples of Asia and the world. It would seem that the Lord of the Harvest has been pleased to use APTS as a major factor in sustaining continuity and stability within the Assemblies of God throughout the Asia Pacific region over these past forty years. While there have been many contributing factors to the dynamic growth, influence and strength of the various national Assemblies of God fellowships in the region, APTS surely has had a significant place. Governed by a dozen national Assemblies of God general councils that border the Pacific Rim in partnership with the American Assemblies of God World Missions (AGWM), APTS is truly a shared vision and ministry.

In the pages that follow, we will take a journey through the story of this remarkable school during the first forty years of its existence. We will review its origins and trace its process through both humble years and those with more dramatic developments, to the present. With the completion in 2001 of a major new facility, the Asia Pacific Center for the Advancement of Leadership and Missions (APCALM), an edifice that is primarily intended to facilitate the equipping of Spirit-filled Asians and Pacific Islanders for missionary ministry, APTS is poised to provide even greater service in the 21st Century.

The Birth of an Idea

God Sends Revival

The beginning of the modern Pentecostal revival is considered by many scholars to have been on New Year's Day 1901. It was in the Midwestern American town of Topeka, Kansas that an unusual outpouring of the Spirit occurred in an informal short-term Bible school operated by an earnest Holiness minister, Charles F. Parham. Students began to experience the Baptism in the Holy Spirit, accompanied by speaking in other tongues as the Spirit gave utterance (Acts 2:1-4). To be sure, before this event, there had been others in various parts of the world who had reported similar phenomena, but it was at Parham's Bethel Bible School that a connection was made between the experience of the Spirit-baptism and speaking in tongues as the initial physical evidence of the experience. This is what gave theological identity to the burgeoning Pentecostal movement.

From Topeka, the story moved to Los Angeles, where in 1906, in a humble meeting place on Azusa Street, the Pentecostal revival became known around the world. Rapidly it became an international movement. Speaking in tongues and the expectation that the gifts of the Spirit enumerated in 1 Corinthians 12 were available to the contemporary church led to widespread ostracism, scorn, and outright persecution of adherents of the revival movement. In spite of well-nigh universal rejection, the movement flourished. From early days, wise leaders insisted that the Word of God must judge all spiritual phenomena.

This emphasis on the teaching of Scripture was an important key to providing stability to the revival movement and, in time, led to a strong commitment to the value of Bible institutes as an important means for providing biblically trained pastors and missionaries. The Assemblies of God in America, just one of many Pentecostal groups, led the nation's denominations in the development of Bible schools around the world. Increasingly, sister Assemblies of God organizations in many parts of the world provided for their leadership by developing their own Bible schools.

The Revival Spreads to Asia

In the Asia Pacific region, the message of the empowering of the Spirit came in a variety of ways over a period of years. From the beginnings of the modern Pentecostal revival, a hallmark was evangelism and missions. From Azusa Street, Spirit-filled believers were called to diverse nations, often going out without any sending agency or promise of financial support. Gradually, the American Assemblies of God developed an orderly program for endorsing, supporting and directing the activities of those whom God had called for overseas cross-cultural ministries. Other Pentecostal bodies, both in the USA and Europe, did likewise. In the 1920s and 1930s, a trickle of pioneer missionary activity brought sparks of Pentecostal revival to various Asian and Pacific Island nations. Sometimes, in the period before World War II, the first ones to bring the Pentecostal message to Asian nations were native citizens who had gone abroad for employment. One such example is Rudy Esperanza, first general superintendent of the Philippines General Council of the Assemblies of God (PGCAG), who found Christ as Savior in the State of Washington as a Filipino worker abroad. The Lord led him to return to his homeland to become a pioneer in the Pentecostal revival among his own people. Today, the PGCAG is reported to be the largest Evangelical body in the nation, with over three thousand local churches.

The fascinating stories of the pioneers who first planted the message of the "Full Gospel" disclose a pattern of individuals, called by God, who usually endured considerable opposition and worked with very limited resources. The dislocations caused by World War II in the

Pacific temporarily brought the expansion of Pentecostal ministry to a halt. It was after the war that growth in many Pacific Rim lands began to accelerate.

The Need for Training is Recognized

A common pattern of pioneer missionary endeavor in those early years was to plant churches and identify potential young national leaders. The nurturing of these leaders led inevitably to the formation of Bible schools. Some of these efforts were certainly quite modest, amounting to little more than amplified Sunday school programs but, eventually, many Bible institutes caught hold as the value of their alumni became readily apparent. Often these schools took on the institutional forms that missionaries brought, chiefly from the USA. This meant the cultivation of adequate faculty, the erection of living accommodations for residential students, the development of appropriate curricula and the gathering of sufficient books and periodicals to supply libraries. Emphasis on cultivating a strong spiritual life and organized field ministry rounded out the life of these early Bible school students. Missionaries usually served in a part-time capacity as the teachers of these early schools. Gradually however, it became more and more apparent that the goal of developing a truly indigenous national church meant that administration and teaching in the Bible schools should be placed more and more in the hands of the national leaders. This, naturally, raised the question of how these national school faculty would themselves be educated.

The Vision of Maynard Ketcham

By the late 1950s, Maynard Ketcham, field secretary for the Far East of the American Assemblies of God, recognized that an advanced school located in Asia was sorely needed. Observation disclosed that promising leaders who were sent to non-Pentecostal institutions often returned with views at variance with Pentecostal teaching and, thus, were rendered unsuitable to train Pentecostal young people for ministry. In addition, the experience of some mission organizations indicated that sending Asian young people to study in the West often resulted in their settling in the West instead of returning to their homelands in Asia. Citing statistics from a study by Jim Davis, a missionary, Ketcham reported that only 37 percent of Assemblies of God students going to the West for study returned to their countries of origin for ministry. Consequently, he set his sights on the establishment of a strong advanced Bible school in Asia to serve the growing needs of the Assemblies of God churches in the region.

Humble Beginnings: (1960-1964)

Planning for an Advanced School

At the September 1960 Far East Conference of the American Assemblies of God Foreign Missions Department held in Hong Kong, Maynard Ketcham appealed for an advanced Bible school to serve the growing needs of the region. At that time, the Far East Assemblies of God operated sixteen Bible schools, graduating approximately 150 students each year. These schools offered one-, two- or three-year programs. The need for qualified faculty and administrators was clear. At the conference, representatives from Korea, Japan, Taiwan, Hong Kong, Indonesia, Malaysia, Burma, and the Philippines discussed Ketcham's proposal and approved the creation of the Far East Advanced School of Theology (FEAST). FEAST was intended to offer the additional years of study needed for students to obtain a bachelor's degree. It was agreed that such a school should be located in Manila, and Ketcham was authorized to secure a qualified leader who would shepherd the implementation of this plan.

Harold Kohl, who had served as a missionary to Ceylon (Sri Lanka) and was then pastoring in East Brunswick, New Jersey, was moved upon in an unusual outpouring of the Spirit in his church one Sunday evening in 1962. He and his wife, Beatrice, concluded that God wanted them to return to foreign missions service. Kohl called his friend Maynard Ketcham to inquire into the current missions needs. Several days later, Ketcham shared with the Kohls his vision for an advanced

Bible school in the Far East and invited them to consider shouldering the responsibility of opening the new institution. After prayer, Harold and Bea Kohl accepted the invitation, arriving in Manila in March 1963.

Secretary Ketcham invited the respective national Assemblies of God general councils to send representatives to a meeting designed to plan the shape of the proposed new school. The Far East Bible School Administrative Committee (FEBSAC) was formed at this time, with Harold Kohl serving as chair. Representatives from Korea, Malaysia, the Philippines and the Marshall Islands constituted the others on the committee. A central objective of FEBSAC was to secure an integration of the curricula of the various Far East Bible schools, since it was clear that such coordination was necessary as a basis upon which to add an advanced school program. They agreed upon a brief statement outlining the objectives of the school, some guidelines for the curriculum, and student admission policies. Only those holding ministerial credentials were to be accepted, with each applicant required to have the endorsement of his or her general council. Kohl remembers that in most cases there was good cooperation, though some questioned the advisability of offering anything beyond the typical three-year Bible institute program. There was even opposition in some cases. History shows that revival movements often encounter a degree of ambivalence toward higher education, an attitude born of fear that too much education might hinder the work of the Holy Spirit and engender pride. In the early years, the faculty and administration of FEAST had to work hard to convince the reluctant that earnest and extended study of the Bible really was, after all, beneficial for furthering the work of the kingdom of God.

It was agreed that the new school should be located at the front of the compound that housed Bethel Bible Institute (BBI) in Manila, Valenzuela, a suburb of Manila. The reasons articulated for this decision included the strength of the Assemblies of God in the Philippines (with over 400 churches), the existence of four Bible institutes that could serve as "feeder" schools, the wide use of English, and the status of the Philippines as a Christian nation. A building was designed to house a maximum of forty students. This modest proposal was based on the assumption that FEAST would also offer a program of on-site extension classes in various countries, in effect, taking the school to the students. In addition, it was expected that some students would commute to that school from the greater Manila area. These factors led to the decision to erect a modest structure to serve the perceived needs of the new school.

By now, Kohl was able to outline in clear fashion the objectives of FEAST. He started his understanding of the mission of FEAST as follows:

1. To encourage fidelity to God's written word and increased spiritual development in faculty and students.
2. To develop excellence in Christian ministry.
3. To establish a center from which to help elevate ministerial/theological education throughout the Asia Pacific region.
4. To establish a series of locations in the region as extension centers of FEAST "to bring the school to the students."
5. To educate and train a much-needed core of able teachers and administrators for the Bible schools in the region.
6. To assist God-called men and women in developing their gifts and talents for pastoral, evangelistic, missionary and leadership ministries in their national churches.
7. To create opportunities for cross-cultural understanding and international friendships that would lead to greater interaction and cooperation in joint ventures for the strengthening and expansion of Christ's church in the affected region.

FEAST Begins Operation

FEAST began its first year of operation on July 29, 1964. Seventeen students had applied, but only six were accepted. The first classes met in the office of Kohl on the campus of BBI, since he also was serving as president of that institution. There was no library, so the resources of BBI were required to support the work of the first classes. Bea Kohl, serving as librarian, developed the FEAST library. On October 13, 1964, a groundbreaking ceremony was held for the first phase of the FEAST administrative building.

Beginning in 1964, the Boys and Girls Missionary Crusade (BGMC) of the American Assemblies of God contributed a substantial amount of money to support the development of the FEAST library. Faithfully over the years, BGMC has continued to contribute regularly to augment the library resources, with the total supplied now amounting to well over $400,000. During the course of the first year, the initial phase of the FEAST building project was undertaken.

Working with the president and the academic dean in that initial year was Derrick Hillary, an Assemblies of God missionary colleague living in Manila who served as dean of students. In those early years, Kohl filled the role of business manager as well. It was a humble beginning, but FEAST was in operation. The dream of Maynard Ketcham was now a reality.

The Early Years: (1965-1972)

A Home for the School

Work proceeded slowly on the FEAST structure since construction could be undertaken only as funds were available. The first stage of construction was completed debt-free within one year and the building was ready for the second year of the school's operation.

On May 6, 1965, following the conclusion of the initial year of classes, the first phase of the FEAST building was dedicated with Rudy Esperanza, general superintendent, as the speaker. Over the next seven years, the building was completed in two more stages, funded largely by generous support from American churches.

Harold Kohl reports that during the second stage of construction funds had run out and the uncompleted building was left exposed, both to the weather and to the very real possibility of theft. Classroom equipment, dormitory furnishings, library materials, office equipment and other appliances were at risk. With the school term nearing an end, the campus would soon be empty of students who served as guards. During a chapel service, Kohl presented the need to the students and faculty—$5,000 for materials and labor to enclose the building. Time was spent in the chapel hour in intercession for this need, with the faculty and students specifically praying for $5,000. The next morning Kohl received a letter from Maynard Ketcham stating that someone had sent him a check in the amount of $5,000, requesting that it would be used where most needed in the Far East. Brother Ketcham had been impressed to write to Harold Kohl asking if he had need for this money! When the students gathered for the next chapel service, it was Kohl's joy to report how God had answered their prayer within twenty-four hours! He admonished the students to carry with them this testimony as they entered various posts of ministry to remember God's faithfulness in times of crisis.

Foreign Students Arrive

Kohl spent many hours in government offices over the course of many months in an attempt to secure government permission to enroll foreign students for theological studies. This task, which entailed numerous visits to the departments of Education and Immigration, occupied the president for the better part of a year. Because of these efforts, in 1965, students from foreign lands began to arrive.

The Academic Program Develops

The initial degree offering of FEAST was the Bachelor of Theology (B.Th.), a program requiring two years of residence. Because the school was deemed a religious institution, the Philippine government advised that the school's board of directors could authorize the granting of the appropriate degrees since such academic programs did not fall within the jurisdiction of the Philippine government. Consequently, in 1966, the Foreign Missions Committee (FMC) of the American Assemblies of God, which constituted the FEAST board of directors, authorized the granting of both the B.Th. and Bachelor of Religious Education (B.R.E.) degrees.

Help Arrives!

In 1965, Trinidad Esperanza, sister of Rudy Esperanza, general superintendent, and a recent graduate of Fuller Theological Seminary, joined the FEAST team as registrar. Trinidad (later married to Romulus Seleky, a FEAST graduate from Indonesia) served for many years as an effective faculty member and administrator of the school and was dearly beloved by all. She was concurrently the treasurer of the PGCAG for much of this time. Over the years, Trinidad Seleky made numerous trips to various parts of the Philippines representing the interests of FEAST with passion and effectiveness. She went to be with the Lord in January 1995.

During the late 1960s and early 1970s, several missionaries came to augment the staff of FEAST. Among these were Dr. Koichi and Ellen Kitano, Dr. George and Roberta Batson, and Phyllis Bakke from the USA. Dr. Koichi Kitano initially served as business administrator and then as academic dean from 1973 to 1976. He was also dean of students at various times in the late 1970s and mid-1980s. The Philippine faculty included Eleazar Javier (later to serve as general superintendent of the PGCAG) and Lorenzo Lazaro. Felicidad Sato (1969) served as librarian.

In 1968, while Kohl and his wife were on a two-year fund-raising furlough, Derrick Hillary was acting president. He invited James and Velma Long to transfer from Iloilo City to FEAST. James Long was requested to serve as business manager and dean of students. A major early contribution of James Long was the supervision of the completion of the second phase of the FEAST building. A chapel, additional classrooms and library were added in this contribution project. Maynard Ketcham allocated $10,000 to provide for the completion of the FEAST building. When the building was completed, Thomas F. Zimmerman, general superintendent of the American Assemblies of God, came to be the dedication speaker. Philip Hogan, the executive director of the American Assemblies of God missions department, also attended this significant ceremony.

Early Graduates

On April 22, 1966, two students, Tommy Reyes and Jaime Marcos, constituted the first graduating class of FEAST. (See Appendix A for a list of all APTS graduates projected through 2023.)

Among those graduating in the second class (1967) was Virginia (Virgie) Cruz. Cruz for many years distinguished herself in creative and pioneer evangelistic and pastoral ministries, becoming recognized as one of the outstanding Evangelical leaders in the Philippines. She was a strong supporter of her alma mater, serving for many years on the board of the Theological Foundation of Asia (TFA), the Philippine corporation that holds title to the property of APTS. (Virginia Cruz died in an automobile accident in the USA in 1999.) Also graduating in 1967 was the first non-Filipino student, Gideon Nair, from Fiji.

An early graduate of FEAST was Cresmerio Fernandez (1968). He and his wife, Norma (1973), became the first foreign missionaries appointed by the PGCAG, accepting a call to serve in war-torn Vietnam. Following ministry in the provinces, they and their small daughter barely escaped during the fall of Saigon. Unable to return to Vietnam, the Fernandez family served for some years as missionaries in Singapore. From the outset, the vision to train students for foreign missions was high on the FEAST agenda. In the 1990s, Norma Fernandez (1973) served as president of Mindanao Regional Bible College (MRBC) in General Santos City. Another early graduate was Menasse Rumkeny from Indonesia (1971, 1984) who later became the assistant general superintendent of the Indonesia General Council and principal of the Assemblies of God Bible School in Malang, Indonesia.

Asian Seminar of Evangelism and Missions (ASEM)

To promote evangelistic ministry, God sent along missionary Wes Weekley. During the summer of 1971, Evangelist Weekley developed a burden to train national evangelists and missionaries–seeing FEAST as an ideal site for an annual 4-6 week seminar to offer practical training in several areas of evangelistic ministry. This led to the launching of the Asian Seminar of Evangelism and Missions (ASEM) in April and May of 1973. ASEM continued as an annual event until 1979 when FEAST began plans for a master's level program in missions.

Support of Missions Leaders

Maynard Ketcham spearheaded the founding of FEAST and gave it strong support through the remainder of his tenure as field secretary for the Far East. In 1970, he was succeeded by Wesley R. Hurst, who gave unstinting support to FEAST during his entire period of service until his death in 1987. Fittingly, the main administrative building on the present campus was named Hurst Hall.

The FMC in Springfield, serving as the board of directors of FEAST for twenty-five years, proved to be a responsive and supportive source of guidance. These early leaders of FEAST established a strong reputation for academic excellence in spite of many towering obstacles. The quality of the graduates of those early years proved to be persuasive, demonstrating that the time and resources invested in advanced theological education were making a substantial contribution to stable and wise leadership throughout the region. The school motto, Zeal with Knowledge, was clearly more than a mere slogan–it was a true reflection of the philosophy of FEAST.

Years of Consolidation: (1972-1984)

Beginning of the FEAST Extension Program

From the inception of FEAST, the dream had been to implement an extension program that would take the services of the advanced school to strategic locations throughout the region. Such a program would multiply the usefulness of the school, making its services available to many students who could not uproot their lives, families, and ministries to spend extensive time at the Manila campus. In order to make the extension program a reality, it was first necessary to coordinate the curriculum offerings of the existing Bible schools.

An important milestone in the development of the FEAST extension program was the meeting of the Core Curriculum Committee on the FEAST campus in Manila from December 28, 1972 to January 4, 1973. Lester Kenney served as chair and Trinidad Seleky as recording secretary. Harold Kohl, Paul Pomerville, Everett McKinney, William Farrand, Charles Butterfield, Eli Javier and Manuel Monintja were the missionaries and national leaders representing various Asian constituencies. Also participating were Dr. Art Stewart of Washington, Dr. George Flattery and Warren Flattery of ICI, Brussels and Dr. William Menzies of Evangel College, Springfield, Missouri. This working group devised a core curriculum, to be recommended to all participating Bible schools in the region. This agreement was to be the basis for the orderly development of advanced courses, such as those to be provided by the FEAST extension program. With the establishment of appropriate courses at the one-, two-, and three-year levels of Bible school institution, the way was now open for FEAST to provide the fourth- and fifth-year courses through on-site services throughout the region.

The FEAST on-site courses began almost immediately. Initially, the degree of B.A. in Bible was offered, requiring one year of additional academic work beyond the three-year Bible institute diploma. The nomenclature of this degree was changed in 1974 to Bachelor of Biblical Studies (B.B.S.) as required by Philippine law. In March and April 1973, Harold Kohl and George Batson provided the inaugural on-site courses on the campus of the Bible Institute of Malaya (BIM) in Kuala Lumpur. In May 1973, Eli Javier and Trinidad Seleky conducted a FEAST on-site at Immanuel Bible Institute (IBI) in Cebu. In August George Batson and Dr. William Menzies conducted the first on-site in Korea with about sixty pastors enrolled (about half of all the Assemblies of God pastors registered at that time in Korea). Each year thereafter, extension courses were offered in various locations, including a program begun in Fiji in 1974. Augmenting the resident faculty of FEAST were faculty from American Bible schools who offered their services from time to time, as well as Asian national leaders who served alongside their American colleagues.

James Long Becomes the Second FEAST President

During 1973, Harold Kohl, founding president of FEAST, resigned to accept an appointment as dean of the college division of ICI in Brussels, Belgium. James Long, who had been serving as business manager, was asked to add to his responsibilities the role of acting president. For some time, Long served as the president, academic dean and business manager, indicating the severe strain on human resources during these lean years. James Long, ably assisted by his wife, Velma (who went to be with the Lord in July 2003), deferred his passion for pastoral and evangelistic ministry to aid FEAST, knowing that his services were desperately needed. Gradually, additional workers joined the team, but during much of the decade, FEAST was severely understaffed. Long appealed to American Bible school faculty to assist with the growing extension ministry. There were simply not enough full-time faculty to answer all the demands pouring in to FEAST.

Faculty and Staff During 1970s

The Leslie Bedell family joined the FEAST faculty in September 1973. Dr. William Greene, faculty member of Bethany Bible College, Santa Cruz, California, came as visiting professor and later returned for a second brief period of service. Keith Sorbo, the son of missionary parents to Indonesia, taught for three years at FEAST in the mid-1970s. John and Joyce Burnett, William Farrand, Paul Klahr, Gary Denbow and Ruth Waldenmaier were missionaries in the Philippines who provided part-time service. Barbara Johnson, Gary Liddle, John and Juanell Robinson, and Wayne Radford were among those who came to serve FEAST for limited periods of service, as well.

Dr. George Batson was named academic dean in 1976, while Dr. Koichi Kitano served as dean of students from 1977 to 1981. These appointments helped distribute the administrative load that had been borne so long by James Long. For two years, from 1976 to 1978, Wesley Morton of the USA served as a special representative of FEAST among USA churches. He and his wife provided a good pastoral role during their brief stint on campus.

Among staff appointments that are long remembered are Tessie dela Cruz, the president's able secretary, Virginia Palacios (known to many as the "queen of the kitchen") and Thessie Alvior (later to become Thessie Colar). Thessie Colar (1973, 1974) continues to work in the library as the longest-serving employee, now with nearly thirty years of service to the school.

In conjunction with the baccalaureate service held on March 15, 1975, Long conducted a memorial service to honor Derrick Hillary, who had served as FEAST's first dean of students and briefly as interim president during the Kohls furlough. Brother Hillary had gone to be with the Lord just a few days prior to the service.

Extension Faculty

Among the notable achievements of the Longs was their oversight of the rapidly developing extension program that had been initiated in 1973. During these years, faculty members from several institutions in the USA contributed to the program, including Dr. Delmer Guynes, Dr. Anthony Palma and Dr. Del Tarr from the Assemblies of God Graduate School, Dr. William Menzies from Evangel College, John Morar and Dr. Jessie Moon from Central Bible College, Dr. A. E. Strang from Bethany Bible College and Dr. Dan Pecota from Northwest College. The president's report from 1977 indicated that over the first four years of operation, 440 individual students had enrolled in one or more extension courses. In school year 1976-77, thirteen on-site courses were conducted in seven Asia Pacific countries: Fiji, Hong Kong, Japan, Korea, Indonesia, Singapore, and Malaysia.

Everett McKinney Becomes President

At the end of 1976-1977 academic year, Everett McKinney became president of FEAST, arriving in Manila in March. Jim Long continued as business administrator. The McKinneys came to FEAST from Cebu where Everett had served effectively as president of IBI for a number of years. During his tenure there, the campus was substantially developed.

James and Velma Long resigned in December 1978 to accept the pastorate of the International Charismatic Service (ICS), an international fellowship meeting at the Holiday Inn, Manila. Over the years, the Lord blessed the ministry of the Longs in this strategic church setting while they continued to provide encouragement and support to the FEAST family.

The Master's Program Initiated

In August 1978, FEAST instituted the long-awaited master's level program under the leadership of Everett McKinney and Dr. George Batson, who was the academic dean. Two degrees were offered at this time: the Master of Theological Studies (M.T.S.) and the Master of Religious Education (M.R.E.). Dr. William Menzies came to teach the first course in the new program. By this time, the FEAST library had grown to more than five thousand volumes, providing at least minimal resources for conducting a master's level academic enterprise.

Outstanding Graduates of the 1970s

The FEAST classes of the 1970s produced several outstanding graduates: Arthur Pettyjohn (1972) founded the Church of God Bible Academy (now Asian Seminary of Christian Ministries) in Manila. David Sobrepena (1974, 1975) served as general superintendent of the PGCAG and chair of the APTS board of directors. Abraham Visca (1974, 1985) became a missionary to Papua New Guinea and later served as executive director of the Asia Pacific Theological Association (APTA) from 1993 to 2002. Masaki Sasaki (1975, 1976), missions director for the Japan Assemblies of God, distinguished himself for outstanding pioneer missionary effort in the mountains of Northern Luzon. Dr. Simon Chan (1975, 1976), noted Pentecostal scholar at Trinity Theological College of Singapore, was likely the first FEAST alumnus to receive a Ph.D. degree, doing so at the Cambridge University in England. Tomothy Uelese (1977, 1985) served for many years as president of Samoa Bible College in American Samoa and Walter Caput (1977, 1978, 1992, 2004) served as president of Luzon Bible College in the 1990s and early 2000s. Segundino (Cruz) Ladura (1978, 1979, 1989) became president of Mindanao Regional Bible College in General Santos City, Philippines. Although neither completed a FEAST degree, both Caesar (Butch) Conde and Augustine (Gus) Lising, who distinguished themselves as leaders of the charismatic movement in the Philippines, studied in the masters program at FEAST in the late 1970s and early 1980s.

Faculty Additions in the Early 1980s

A growing number of visiting instructors and short-term workers came to assist in both the residence program of FEAST and the expanding network of extension ministries in these years. Among those who came for periods of a year or more were Dr. Alan Snider and his wife, Dale and Katie Flowers, Ken and Meg McComber, Robert and Beverly Soderberg, Dan and Jeanne Anglin, Robert and Joanne Menzies, Gary and Kathryn Long, and Dr. Charles and Mary Clauser. When Bob and Bev Soderberg retired in 1995, they had completed more than thirteen years of full-time service to FEAST/APTS. Bob served not only as a faculty member in Old Testament, but also as dean of students for many years; Bev served as registrar after Trinidad Seleky's health forced her to remain in the lowlands when the school moved to Baguio City.

Barbara Liddle (now Dr. Barbara Cavaness) taught and served as librarian for a number of years. Dwayne Turner and Debbie Menken (now Dr. Deborah Gill) also provided invaluable service. Dr. Gill is remembered for writing the official school song in 1981, sung annually by graduates and alumni (to which a third verse was added in 1997 by Dr. John Carter). Dan Anglin, later to become a director of the Asia Pacific Education Office (APEO), served as academic dean during the first half of 1982 before moving to the USA to work with ICI. David Ohlerking was appointed to serve as director of development in 1982, and Dr. Del and Dolly Tarr taught on campus for an entire semester in the first part of 1983. During most of the decade of the 1980s, noted New Testament scholar, Dr. Gordon Fee, served as an adjunct faculty member, spending a full trimester on campus on a number of occasions. The sacrificial service of many who came for shorter or longer terms greatly enriched the quality of the FEAST program in these years.

The Search for a New Location

During the tenure of Everett McKinney, the resident population of FEAST reached forty students. There was simply no room to accommodate more students, nor space to house faculty and provide offices for them. The compound in which FEAST operated was shared with several other institutions, including Bethel Bible Institute (BBI), Bible School for the Deaf (BID) and the offices of the PGCAG. The printing press of the PGCAG and the ICI warehouse and associated bookstore took up additional space. It was evident that a change in location was necessary if FEAST was to grow.

McKinney undertook a survey of options available for such a move, seeking to obtain opinions from a broad range of constituencies in early 1980. In the course of that school year, he traveled widely throughout the region evaluating possible sites for the future location of the school, even considering a branch campus in another country to augment the Manila facility. It was quickly determined that a single campus was the only practical option and that the Philippines was still the best location for an international school.

Paul Klahr, a missionary, and Virginia Cruz (1967) helped to find a property in the Fairview area of greater Manila. A deposit was made, holding the property until November 1982. This location was eventually rejected in favor of a parcel in the Ortigas area of Metro Manila. A donation of $200,000 for the purchase of this property was provided by Jimmy Swaggart Ministries. In April 1984, a dedication ceremony was conducted, with Wesley Hurst, Far East Field Secretary, officiating. Plans were initiated with the intention of constructing a six-story high-rise edifice.

A team construction specialist under missions appointment from the Division of Foreign Missions (DFM)-USA, consisting of Ed Roberts, Guy Deal and Bill Pottiger, was on site by September. Although a groundbreaking ceremony was held on September 13, 1984, timed so that dignitaries attending the Far East Conference being held in Manila that month could attend, it quickly became apparent to the construction team that the cost to maintain a high-rise facility suitable for international students in a commercial area like Ortigas was not feasible. The air conditioning cost alone was estimated at $10,000 per month, far more than the school could afford. Philip Hogan, executive director of DFM-USA, who had officiated at the Ortigas groundbreaking, readily acknowledged that rethinking the location of FEAST to another site should be undertaken. This required starting anew to find a more suitable property. In the interim, Deal and Pottiger undertook the task of improving the old FEAST facility, creating faculty offices and improving other features of the campus to make it more usable. Additionally, Roberts and his colleagues worked with the administration in scouting out prospective new sites for the school. These efforts culminated in the eventual move of FEAST to Baguio City in 1986.

Everett McKinney Concludes His Service as President

Everett McKinney served as president of FEAST until 1984 when he and Evelyn returned to the USA on furlough and for further education. McKinney distinguished himself for effective representation of FEAST throughout the region and throughout the USA. Under his direction the extension program flowered, aided by the appointment of a network of FEAST extension representatives in seven Asian and Pacific Island nations that provided a useful system for coordinating the program.

By the fall of 1984, FEAST had established a solid reputation for equipping national leaders for Pentecostal ministry throughout the region. Alumni were filling a significant number of posts in the Bible schools in the region, as well as providing leadership for the respective national Assemblies of God church bodies. The addition of graduate-level programs, including the Master of Divinity degree in the 1982-1983 school year, demonstrated the growing maturity of the institution. In spite of cramped quarters and a program that relied too heavily on short-term and visiting instructors, FEAST was making a substantial contribution to the kingdom of God.

Although Everett McKinney did not resume his role as president when they returned to the field in 1985, he and Evelyn continued to serve the school in multiple ways. In more recent years, the McKinneys have ministered in schools and churches in many parts of the world, but their enlarged ministry has not prevented them from continuing as non-resident faculty of APTS. They had not only taught numerous extension courses, but have frequently served at the resident campus, as well. For some years, Everett helped to coordinate the extension program and served for a time as director of development.

From Manila to Baguio City; From FEAST to APTS: (1985-1989)

Leadership Transitions in the Mid-1980s

In August 1984, Dr. William Menzies came to fill the post of president, albeit for only a one-year special assignment. Among his contributions during this year of service was the initiation of a faculty development program (with funds provided by Field Director Wesley Hurst) that resulted in the completion of Ph.D. studies by Robert Menzies, Gary Long and Dr. Wonsuk Ma (1981, 1983). These efforts later bore fruit when Dr. Robert Menzies and Dr. Ma returned for service on the faculty of APTS. At the end of that year, Dr. Bill and Doris Menzies went to Fresno, California, to fulfill a previously-made commitment to work with Dr. Del and Dolly Tarr in the formation of California Theological Seminary (CTS). Bill Menzies assumed the role of vice-president of the new school.

Dr. Koichi Kitano served ably as academic dean in 1983 and 1984, following his return from furlough. In January 1985, two important additions to the FEAST family were Dr. Klaude and Grace Kendrick and Dr. David and May Lim. Dr. Kendrick, respected elder statesman of American Assemblies of God higher education, joined the team as academic dean. Dr. Lim, coming from Western Pentecostal Bible College in British Columbia, assumed the role of dean of students in the spring term. Dr. Robert and Norene Feller, having arrived in August 1984, completed a year of service with the assignment of setting up a computerized accounting system for the school. Kenneth McComber served as business manager at this time, a role he continued until his return to the USA in 1990 to work with APEO. (Ken McComber passed away in November 2003 at the age of eighty-two.) Thelma Pantig became administrative assistant, serving in this role in addition to being the president's secretary. Since 1965, Trinidad Seleky had been faithfully serving as registrar and director of admissions, a role she maintained until the school relocated to Baguio City in 1986.

Asia Graduate School of Theology (AGST) Involvement

In 1985, chiefly through the skillful liaison of Dr. Koichi Kitano, FEAST was invited to be a founding member of the Asia Graduate School of Theology (AGST), a consortium of the Evangelical seminaries of the Philippines. This relationship bore considerable fruit, especially in the 1990s, when Dr. John Carter, the academic dean, took an active role in the organization.

Asian Faculty Development

To ensure that FEAST would enjoy the services of well-trained faculty in the future, a program for Asian faculty development was launched. In July 1985, Wonsuk Ma from Korea, a newly appointed faculty member, was given an 18-month sabbatical to pursue a Th.M. degree at Fuller Theological Seminary. Ma was granted a second study leave in 1992 to complete his Ph.D. degree. His wife, Julie (1983), also engaged in doctoral studies at Fuller during this time. In 1996, both Wonsuk and Julie Ma earned Ph.D. degrees from Fuller and were recognized as the first husband/wife team in Fuller's history to be awarded such degrees in the same commencement ceremony. Dr. Wonsuk Ma's continuing service over the years to FEAST/APTS gives him the distinction of having the longest tenure of ministry on the faculty. Beginning in1996, Dr. Wonsuk Ma filled the post of academic dean while Dr. Julie Ma served as a faculty member in missiology and editor of the *Journal of Asian Mission* (JAM), a publication of AGST.

Asian-American Board Created

Of considerable significance was the appointment in September 1985 of an interim Asian-American board (done at the time of the Eighth East Asian Conference that met in Manila). This transitional board consisted of national church leaders and American Assemblies of God missionaries who agreed to serve until a permanent Asian-American board could be put in place. A new constitution for FEAST was written, replacing the governance of the school by the American Assemblies of God Foreign Missions Committee (FMC) with a regional board of directors, consisting principally of representatives of the respective Assemblies of God general councils of the Pacific Rim nations. This new constitution was approved by the FMC and presented to the various Asia Pacific general councils for ratification. In the document, it was stipulated that when at least seven general councils approved the new constitution, it would be possible to put into effect the new governance structure.

By 1988, enough approvals had been received to announce the implementation of the new governing body effective in March 1989. In this fashion, FEAST, which had been born of American missionary vision and brought along chiefly through the resources of American personnel and finance, now came under the control of Asia Pacific Assemblies of God church leaders who held a majority of seats on the board of directors. American missionary representation continued, to be sure, but in a less significant role from that time onward. It is noteworthy that an increasing proportion of the administration and faculty of the school have come from Asia, thus, becoming a clear illustration of the principle of collegiality and partnership that has been at the heart of the philosophy of the American Assemblies of God foreign missions vision.

Dr. Kendrick Obtains Property for FEAST in Baguio City

In July 1985, when Dr. William and Doris Menzies returned to the USA, Dr. Klaude Kendrick was named president of FEAST and Dr. David Lim was appointed to serve as academic dean. Dr. Kendrick moved swiftly to secure appropriate property for the school, since the urgency to move to better facilities had become critical. On December 26, 1985, a contract was signed for a ten-acre site at the edge of Baguio City. This former corporate retreat center, owned by Philippine First Holdings Corporation, was ideally located and well suited for development to serve the future needs of FEAST. The property contained ten buildings, including eight individual houses that could be adapted for student and faculty housing and other school functions. Moreover, because of the moderate climate of Baguio City, the issue of air conditioning the facilities was avoided.

The Move to Baguio City

Plans for preparing the new site for the needs of FEAST were undertaken at once. Roberts, Deal, and Pottiger arranged for the remodeling of the existing buildings and the construction of two new buildings on the campus. One of these new structures, later named Sampaguita Hall, was to be a two-story block of sixteen apartments for married students. A three-story building to house administrative offices, classrooms, library and the chapel was also designed. These new facilities were intended to provide for a student occupancy of approximately one hundred. Work began at once on the project, with occupancy anticipated within the year. A building fund drive to raise the $750,000 needed for this phase of construction was undertaken and successfully completed under the direction of Field Secretary Wesley Hurst. Upon the move of FEAST from Manila, Bethel Bible College (BBC), the sister institution with which FEAST shared the Manila campus, was given the FEAST building.

In October 1986, Dr. Kendrick directed the move of FEAST from Manila to Baguio City. Since the dedication of the new campus was scheduled for January 1987, the move was undertaken in the middle of a term and during the rainy season—a most courageous enterprise—in order for the campus to be ready for the dedication. Facilities were rented in town to house some of the students since the construction project was not quite finished. The library, which by now had grown to more than eight thousand volumes, required many hours of labor to move and set up for effective operation. Equipment and furnishings

Zeal with Knowledge
The First Sixty Years of FEAST/APTS

Photo Gallery 1

Original FEAST logo

1960 Far East Conference

Meynard Ketcham   Hal and Bea Kohl 1966   Kohl and Ketcham

Ground Breaking FEAST 1964

Gallery 1 31

Early FEAST Students

FEAST Building Under Construction

FEAST Administration Building

Trinidad Esperanza

George Batson and Greek Class

FEAST Instructors 1971

Students of 1966-67

Graduates of 1967

1st Korean on-site 1973

Tommy Reyes 1966

Jaime Marcos

Gideon Nair

Jim and Velma Long

Evelyn and Everett McKinney

Gallery 1 33

1969 Student Body in front of the FEAST Building on the campus of the Bethel Bible Institute

1969 Student Body

1971 Student Body

Abe Visca

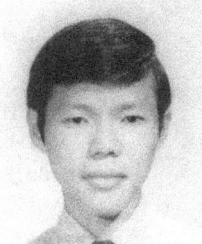

Simon Chan 1971

Bob Soderberg (singing)

Grad Class and Student Body 1974

FEAST Basketball Team 1974

FEAST Faculty 1982

Meg and Ken McComber

Bev Soderberg

Charles and Mary Clauser

Ortigas Ground Breaking

Everett McKinney

Bill Menzies 1985

Klaude Kendrick 1986

Gallery 1   35

Dr David & May Lim

Wonsuk & Julie Ma early 80s

Foreign Missions Commission 1989

Hurst Hall Construction 1986

had to be moved. In spite of rain and poor roads, the move was achieved without a major incident.

Most of the staff remained in Manila, which necessitated the hiring of numerous new staff persons from the Baguio City vicinity. It is noteworthy that many of the staff initially hired during the first year of operation in Baguio City have continued to serve the school faithfully ever since, including Cecilia (Bing) Padilla (food service), Ricky Caput (assistant maintenance supervisor), Ernesto Cawaling (grounds), Robert Ramos (maintenance), Romeo Colar (maintenance), Jessie Dianson (maintenance), Cristina Fanao (housekeeping), Araceli Valdez (housekeeping), Danny hill (grounds), Benjamin (Jimmy) Andrada (maintenance), Joseph Caluza (plant and facilities supervisor), Eleanor Sebiano (business services and personnel manager), and Sharon Lapisac (food service). Thessie (Alvior) Colar, for many years part of the library staff, moved with the school from Manila. In April 2004, she will complete thirty years of continuous service to the school.

In January 1987, a dedication ceremony was conducted on the new campus, with Wesley Hurst officiating. Key Asian leaders, missionaries, and many guests from the USA, including the executive director of DFM-USA, J. Philip Hogan, participated in the gala affair. Students, dressed in native costumes from nine nations, gave tours of the campus. It was announced that the FEAST board of directors had approved the new chapel to be named in honor of J. Philip Hogan. One week later, Wesley Hurst, who became ill immediately following the dedication ceremony, died in Hawaii enroute to his home in Springfield, Missouri. He lived long enough to see the fulfillment of a long—cherished dream—the completion of the permanent campus of FEAST. It seemed fitting to all that the new administration building should be named Hurst Hall in his honor.

Dr. David Lim Becomes President

Immediately following the dedication ceremonies, Dr. Klaude Kendrick returned to the USA, having completed his tour of duty as FEAST president. It was announced at the dedication that Dr. David Lim had been named president-elect to follow Dr. Kendrick. Dr. Lim led the school through its first accreditation process, which led to approval of the APTS M.Div. degree by the Association of Theological Education of South-East Asia (ATESEA), the oldest and most prestigious accrediting association in the region. (It should be noted that Harold Kohl had led FEAST through an accreditation process with the Philippine Association of Bible and Theological Schools [PABATS], a Philippine consortium of Evangelical Bible schools but, apparently, this relationship was never finalized.) Under Dr. Lim's direction, Roberts, who was serving as business administrator, and Deal initiated planning for a major new building on the campus (later named Bethesda Hall) to meet the urgent need for more student housing and faculty offices. Dr. Lim was instrumental in the early stages of fund raising for this project.

In February 1988, Dr. David Lim resigned as president, choosing to return to the faculty. Although he had been in office only one year, he contributed greatly to the strengthening of the school, both spiritually and academically. In addition, he had prepared the groundwork for the new building project that had been approved by the board. Statistics from this era reveal that 87 percent of FEAST graduates were in full-time Christian service, chiefly as instructors in the region's growing number of Bible schools. In July 1990, the Lims accepted a call to pastor Grace Assembly of God in Singapore, a ministry that has grown remarkably in the intervening years. Dr. Lim continues to serve as pastor of this congregation and ministers at APTS periodically as a visiting professor and speaker.

Outstanding Graduates of the 1980s

There were many outstanding graduates of FEAST during the 1980s: Derek Tan (1980, 1982) is president of Theological Centre for Asia (TCA) in Singapore and general secretary of the Asia Theological Association (ATA). Dr. Wonsuk Ma (1981, 1983) serves as academic dean of APTS. Yan Leng Pang (1982, 1984) serves as principal of Asia Theological College in Singapore. Jeong Yull Park (1985) served as president of Soon Shin University in Seoul, Korea (now Hansei University). Naomi Dowdy (1985), who graduated from the Singapore on-site, is pastor of Trinity Christian Centre, one of the largest Assemblies of God churches in Singapore. Roslim Suwandoko

(1985) graduated from the Indonesia on-site and later became general superintendent of the Indonesia Assemblies of God. Terrence Sinnadurai (1986, 1997), who graduated from both the Malaysia on-site and resident campus, served for many years as principal of Malaysia Tamil Bible Institute (MTBI) in Kuala Lumpur, Malaysia. Dr. Joseph Suico (1987) is APTS dean of students. Jong-Guk Kim (1988, 1992) is co-founder and president of Full Gospel Whitestone Mission Bible College in Tarlac City, Philipines. Felipe Acena (1988) served as general secretary of PGCAG for many years. Elena Castillo (1988) is president of the Bible Institute for the Deaf (BID) in Manila. Hariagus Rimba (1988) pastors a large church in Jakarta, Indonesia and is a member of the APTS advisory council. Arun Sarkar (1989) is vice president of Buntain Theological College in Calcutta, India. Anuparp Wichitnantana (1989) is general superintendent of the Assemblies of God of Thailand.

The Decade of Harvest: The 1990s and Early 2000s

Dr. William Menzies Returns as President

Upon the resignation of Dr. Lim, an invitation was extended to Dr. William Menzies to become the president of FEAST. Dr. Menzies, who had previously served on a one-year special assignment as president in 1984-85, accepted the invitation. In May 1988, he and his wife, Doris, were given missionary appointment by DFM-USA and commenced the process of deputation required of new candidates. The Menzies arrived in Baguio City in March 1989, in time for the first meeting of the new Asian-American board of FEAST. The new board included Prince Guneratnam (general superintendent of the Assemblies of God of Malaysia), chair; Robert Houlihan (DFM), vice-chair; Akiei Ito (general superintendent of Japan Assemblies of God), secretary; and Jon Pineda (general superintendent of Micronesia Assemblies of God), treasurer. This original slate of board officers continued without interruption until 1994, providing strong, wise, and stable leadership to the school. Also on the board from the beginning was Alfred Ang from Singapore, who served continuously from 1989 to 2001 including a period as chair from 1995 to 2001.

New Faculty Arrive

Arriving along with the Menzies in 1989 were Dr. Mel and Martha Ming and their family, and Dr. Jack and Adel Rozell. Dr. Ming had previously been serving as academic dean at Northwest College in Kirkland, Washington, and Dr. Rozell, who was trained and certified as a marriage and family counselor, had served for over twenty years as a pastor in Bellevue, Washington. Their coming significantly strengthened the faculty resources of the school.

These three families shared a calling to full-time missions ministry fairly late in life. The ministry experience they brought with them added a degree of maturity to the already well-qualified and competent faculty. Dr. Mel Ming assumed the post of academic dean, a role he filled with enthusiasm and expertise until his return to the USA in 1991. Among his important achievements during this two-year tenure was the recruiting of Joseph Suico (1987) and Roli dela Cruz (1990), both from the Philippines, and Norma Lam (1991) from Malaysia to join the Asian faculty development program. All three eventually completed doctoral study and contributed greatly to the seminary. Dr. Jack Rozell brought a strong commitment to practical ministry, not only to the academic programs of the school, but by constantly looking for creative ways to extend opportunities for ministry by the APTS family to the surrounding communities.

FEAST Becomes APTS

In the fall of 1989, the board agreed to a change in the name of the institution since the expression "Far East" employed in "FEAST" was perceived to reflect a colonial terminology and the preferred reference for the region had become "Asia Pacific." Consequently, the school became Asia Pacific Theological Seminary (APTS). This terminology also accurately reflected the predominantly graduate level of the institution.

New Facilities are Constructed

Since Ed Roberts, the director of construction on the first phase of buildings at the Baguio City campus, found it necessary to return to USA in early 1989, a decision was made to place the responsibility for the construction of the new campus facility in the care of Guy Deal, an engineer. Deal, working with a crew of over one hundred men, supervised the design and the construction work on the new dormitory and office complex, an endeavor that took nearly two years. The Bethesda Foundation of Colorado Springs, Colorado, contributed very substantially to this project, leading the board to assign the name Bethesda Hall to this imposing and functional four-story building. At the same time, it was decided to build a second, smaller, apartment building to serve the anticipated increase in married students. This unit was eventually named Esperanza Hall to honor the first Assemblies of God general superintendent of the Philippines, Rudy Esperanza. A groundbreaking ceremony was conducted in December 1989, with the completed structures being dedicated in March 1991. Altogether, this phase of campus development was valued at $750,000.

The Great Baguio City Earthquake

On July 16, 1990, Baguio City was struck by a major earthquake measuring 7.7 on the Richter scale. Bethesda Hall, with construction well under way, survived the massive tremors without serious damage. The engineers had designed the building well! On campus were some broken pipes and cracks that appeared in some walls, but it was determined that, except for the pelota court, one of the original campus structures, none of the buildings had suffered major damage. This facility, used for both athletic activity and storage, required major rebuilding to prevent its collapse. Many of the retaining walls on campus had been badly damaged and required reconstruction. It was estimated that the cost of repairing damage to the campus was in the neighborhood of $50,000. Considering the major devastation to structures throughout Baguio City, including the collapse of the Hyatt Terraces Hotel only a few miles from campus, the limited damage to campus structures can only be considered a miracle of God's protection.

Baguio City was completely cut off from the lowlands by landslides on all the roads leading to the city and telephone communication had been severed. The earthquake occurred during the rainy season, compounding the misery of thousands of people, not only in Baguio City, but also in the outlying villages scattered through the mountain region. The campus population was mobilized to provide relief for the neighboring communities in the form of medical services and housing kits prepared by the construction crew. Spiritual ministry bathed these humanitarian endeavors.

The Ministry Development Program (MDP) is Established

Following the earthquake, Dr. Jack Rozell and his wife, Adel, were instrumental in establishing a regular schedule of ministry to suffering villages in the region, an effort that proved to be so effective that it was later formalized within the seminary structure as the Ministry Development Program (MDP), now known as the Impact Ministry Program. In subsequent years, MDP became a major component of seminary life, providing an avenue of active ministry for students, faculty and staff persons who wished to be involved in practical Christian ministry to the surrounding region. A major purpose of these efforts was to provide ministry models for the students that could be taken back to their own lands. MDP continues as a channel through which up to five container loads of Christian literature and medical supplies, shipped through World Opportunities International of Hollywood, CA, are received each year from donors in the USA and distributed to hundreds of churches in the Cordillera region. For a number of years, the cost of these container shipments has been covered through donations from International Christian Assembly (ICA) in Hong Kong.

Other ministries of MDP have included a weekly ministry at the Baguio City jail, monthly medical/evangelicalism/counselling (MEC) outreaches to the villages of Northern Luzon using medical supplies received in the container shipments or purchased locally, children's evangelism ministries, pastors' seminars, and Bible teaching programs in local schools. These ministries, undertaken in cooperation with local Assemblies of God churches, have resulted in many commitments to Christ each month. When the health of Adel made it necessary for the Rozells to return to the USA in 1995, Dr. Norma Lam, faculty member from Malaysia from 1991 to 2001, assumed responsibility for the administration of MDP ministries. From the mid-1990s, missionaries Anita Swartz and Adeline Ladera from the Philippines have served with MDP, providing essential continuity to its various programs. In

2002, Harold Cole, veteran missionary to Thailand and the Philippines, joined the APTS administration as MDP director.

The Library Advances

Gary and Glenna Flokstra arrived in Manila in August 1986, just in time to participate in the enormous campus move to Baguio City. Flokstra served as head librarian until 1996, when the family found it necessary to relocate to the USA. During his term of service, the APTS library grew to more than thirty thousand volumes, making it one of the outstanding theological libraries in all Southeast Asia. Flokstra also developed a ministry of mentoring librarians in the Bible schools in the region and assisting them in library development. Through his efforts, the library holdings of several of these schools were substantially improved. To encourage cooperation among the theological schools of the Baguio City area, he was founding president of the Baguio-Benguet Theological Library Association. He also served a term as president of the Philippine Theological Library Association. After their departure from APTS, Gary and Glenna Flokstra continued to contribute to the development of the APTS library through making available the services of the Africa Library Services Office (ALSO), of which Gary was then the director. Most library acquisitions and textbooks used by APTS continue to be processed with the assistance of the Flokstras.

After 1996, a series of committed and capable librarians served APTS, building on the strong foundation laid by the Flokstras. These include Melany Wilks (1999), who served as library coordinator from 1996 to 2000, and Nina Coley (2000), who served in this role from 2000 to 2001. Berniece Scroggs came to APTS in 2001 as head librarian. During these years, the Asia Pacific Research Center (APRC) was also established to give special emphasis to acquiring archive materials and resources on Asian Pentecostal history, including the oral histories of the founding missionaries and pastors of Assemblies of God of the region.

During the 1990s, the library holdings were initially computerized with the installation of an Online Public Access System (OPAC). In 2000 to 2003, a more advanced computer cataloging system was installed (Alexandria), providing for the use of barcodes for inventory management and checkout and, in 2002, a 3M magnetic strip security system was installed. By 2004, total library holdings had grown to over sixty thousand volumes and other resources. The APTS library continues to be prized as a most valuable center for research and study. However, library space to house the continually growing collection and serve an increasing student population has nearly been exhausted, requiring plans for expanded facilities in the near future.

New Academic Leadership

In 1991, when the Dr. Mel Ming family returned to the USA, Dr. John and Bea Carter responded to the invitation to join the APTS team. The Carters had been working with ICI in Brussels, Belgium, where John was dean of the college. With a Ph.D. in Educational Psychology and experience in a variety of academic settings, Dr. Carter's background gave him excellent preparation for his new role as academic dean with APTS. Prior to missions appointment, he had taught in the School of Education at Syracuse University in Syracuse, New York, worked as a civilian research psychologist at the U.S. Navy Personnel Research and Development Center in San Diego, California, and served for two years as an educational consultant to Educational Radio and Television of Iran in Tehran. He also taught at Southern California College (now Vanguard University) in Costa Mesa, California, between two terms of service at ICI.

Bea Carter found her ministry in reviewing and helping students edit their papers for correct English before they were submitted to their professors. She also loved hosting student wives and children in their home, teaching them to cook American food and learning from them to cook theirs. As such, she enjoyed the informal title "campus grandma."

The Carters were nearing the end of their term with ICI when, in early 1991, it was announced that the ministry would move its headquarters from Brussels to the USA later that year. Although the Carters had no specific direction at that point as to where they would go, they felt a definite leading to remain in ministry overseas. About this same time, Dr. Mel Ming submitted his resignation as APTS academic dean. When it became known that the Carters were open to another assignment, Bob Houlihan, field director for Asia Pacific, called to ask if they would consider moving to APTS. After a time of prayer, and feeling that this was from God, they enthusiastically accepted this invitation, moving to Baguio City in July 1991.

Dr. Carter employed his administrative and teaching skills with distinction, both as academic dean and an outstanding classroom instructor. He also contributed to the ongoing development of AGST, the Philippine network of Evangelical seminaries of which APTS was a founding member. Following its initial development under the leadership of Dr. Mel Ming, Dr. Carter directed the first AGST program to be sponsored and supervised on the APTS campus. This program led to the Th.M. and D.Min. degrees in Pastoral Ministries. It is noteworthy that the D.Min. program operated by APTS and AGST from 1991 to 1996 was the first doctoral program offered at any Assemblies of God institution. Two APTS faculty members, Joseph Suico and Norma Lam, earned Th.M. degrees through AGTS and Norma Lam went on to complete her D.Min. degree in the program.

Dr. John Carter's larger responsibilities to the region included service to the Asia Pacific Theological Association (APTA), a fellowship of more than eighty Asia Pacific Bible schools. From 1991 until the present, he has served as the chair of the accreditation commission of APTA, giving leadership to the development of its accreditation process, and from 1997 to 2000, he was chair of the board of APTA.

Campus Improvement Projects

Although the annual rainfall in Baguio City averages 150 inches, there is a serious water supply shortage in the area during the dry season. The problem of uneven distribution of rainfall through the course of the year, marked by a dry season and a wet season, is compounded by the extensive deforestation in the upland areas. During the early years on the Baguio City campus, the water supply was typically running very low by the end of the academic year in March, so little activity could be supported on campus from March until July. This raised questions about the future development of the campus and its programs. Initially only one deep well was available to serve the needs of the school. In the course of time, a second large water tank at the top of the campus was installed, a second well drilled, and a stream running through the campus tapped to provide extra water resources. These improvements made it possible to think in larger terms about campus utilization, including the development of on-campus programs in the dry season.

In addition to the potential water supply problem, the campus suffered uncertain electric power from the local utility company. During severe typhoons, the campus frequently experienced extended "brownouts." To compensate for this, a large generator was installed to provide essential power to the main campus building in emergencies so that the ongoing school activities could proceed with a degree of normalcy. An on-campus chlorination and filtration system also were installed to ensure that the water on campus was safe for consumption.

Missions Training Programs are Developed

With water and power resources improved, it became possible to utilize the campus for a variety of summer programs. The first such program, the Asian Institute for Media Ministries (AIMM) was offered in 1991. AIMM was developed under the leadership of Bill Snider, Director of AP2000 (now called APMedia), the Assemblies of God media ministry for the region, and APTS faculty member Ian Henderson from Australia. Subsequent AIMM programs were offered in alternate years through 1997. Aided by scholarship grants, promising young people from Mongolia, New Caledonia, Papua New Guinea, and many other nations have attended AIMM to develop skills in radio, TV and print media.

In 1996, missionaries Ty and Cina Silva initiated a program in cooperation with APTS for equipping national leaders for university campus and youth ministries. The Asian Institute of Youth Studies (AIYS) was repeated in 2000, attracting a significant number of enthusiastic young people with a burden to minister to the great university population of Asia Pacific. AIYS is scheduled again for 2004.

The Assemblies of God Asian Missions Association (AGAMA) instituted a bold new plan in 1995 for training Asian believers for cross-cultural missions. Australian Assemblies of God missions training director, Kevin Hovey, working in conjunction with Eu Yat Wan, AGAMA executive director from Singapore, developed a highly successful eight-week missions training program (MTP) that has been offered annually at APTS during the summer break period since 1997. AGAMA recognized that APTS is located strategically for cross-cultural missions training purposes since the campus is within a short distance of tribal villages where direct missions ministry can be experienced by the students. It is noteworthy that an increasing number of APTS graduates are entering cross-cultural missions ministry as a long-term commitment.

A significant development during the mid-1990s was the initiation of the Institute of Islamic Studies (IIS) in 1998. When Hariagus Rimba, an Assemblies of God pastor from Jakarta, Indonesia and APTS alumnus, attended the first meeting of the APTS advisory council in 1994, he encouraged the seminary to consider the development of an Islamic Studies Center on campus. Giving substance to his suggestion, his church contributed $20,000 toward this purpose and has continued to support IIS in subsequent years.

Melvin Ho, an APTS faculty member from Malaysia who served from 1992 to 2002, was asked by Dr. Menzies to provide ideas for developing plans for such a program. Later, Dr. John Carter enlisted the assistance of Ron Peck, executive director of the Center for Ministry to Muslims (CMM) of the USA Assemblies of God, in this endeavor. Peck enthusiastically offered the services of CMM in cooperation with APTS, agreeing to assist in recruiting faculty and support the development of the needed library resources. He asked a member of his staff, Dale Fagerland, to work with APTS. Through these efforts, the first eight-week IIS was conducted on the APTS campus in April to May 1998 as a joint program of APTS, CMM, and AGAMA. Very likely this was the first program of its kind to be offered anywhere in the world.

IIS has continued to be conducted annually, with total enrollment reaching 101 for the 2003 Institute. From the beginning, Dr. Phil Parshall, noted author and Islamic scholar, assisted as a faculty member and enthusiastic promoter of IIS, encouraging many from Evangelical missions agencies to attend. Missionary Mike Langford (2004) presently serves as IIS director.

Faculty Development in the 1990s

For some years, there had been an earnest desire to alter the balance in the administration and faculty of APTS so that a true partnership would emerge between Asian and Western missionaries. During the 1990s, the desired pattern rapidly took shape, so that at the end of the decade there were fourteen missionary faculty members representing nine nations! Among these were Dr. Norma Lam from Malaysia, Dr. Kay Fountain (1994, 1995) from New Zealand, and Dr. Joseph Suico, Dr. Roli dela Cruz and Dr. Lemuel Engcoy (1980, 1985, 1998) from the Philippines, all of whom were participants the APTS faculty development program. Norma Lam received her D.Min. degree from AGST in 1995. Kay Fountain, a missionary from New Zealand, completed a Ph.D. at the University of Auckland in 1999. Assistance was provided to Joseph Suico and Roli dela Cruz to pursue doctoral programs in the United Kingdom. Dr. Suico completed his Ph.D. in 2003 and dela Cruz is expected to finish in 2004. In 2000, Lemuel Engcoy joined the Faculty Development Program, serving as assistant dean of students while pursuing a Doctor of Education (Ed.D.) degree in Pastoral Counseling through AGST in Manila. His wife, Dr. Rose Engcoy (1998, 2003), served as assistant director for the Asia Pacific Research Center (APRC). In 2003, Chang-Soo Kang from Korea, who was completing Ph.D. studies through the APTS/University of Wales program, was appointed as a part-time faculty member.

Looking forward, it is expected that Tham Wan Yee (1986, 2004), missionary from Malaysia, will join the faculty in 2004, having completed the APTS Th.M. degree. Hirokatsu Yoshihara from Japan, who has already served for several years as the instructor for basic Greek courses, will join the faculty development program following the completion of his M.Div. degree in 2004. Through these steps, APTS has begun to realize its long-term goal of establishing a truly coactive partnership with the churches of Asia in the operation of the seminary.

Of particular significance in the development of a multi-national faculty was the issue of how they would be supported. Among the possibilities, of course, was to simply hire qualified Asian faculty. But this would have significantly increased the burden on the school's budget and violated the principle that the operation of APTS was to be a partnership between the Asia Pacific general councils and American missions. Consequently, the approach adopted was that all administrators and faculty should be appointed and supported as missionaries from a national or local church body. In view of the merging strength of the mission programs of many Assemblies of God churches and general councils of the region, this seemed to be a viable approach, and has proven to be so through the ensuing years. Through the decade of the 1990s and early 2000s, APTS has been blessed by the ministry of missionary faculty whose countries of origin have included the Philippines, Malaysia, Korea, New Zealand, Myanmar, Thailand, Japan, Canada, South Africa, and the USA. While it can be noted that some of the missionaries of Asian origin who have served at APTS were appointed by Assemblies of God World Missions (AGWM)-USA (formerly DFM-USA) and drew support from American churches, others were appointed and fully supported by an Asian national church. Nor does this detract from the multi-national character of the APTS faculty. Moreover, this approach has had the benefit of ensuring that all faculty members serve APTS as an expression of their own calling to its ministry, rather than out of the necessity for employment since, as missionaries, they could easily go elsewhere. Undoubtedly, this factor has contributed to the high level of harmony experienced among the APTS faculty through the years, despite the evident cultural differences.

At the end of the 1990s, three of the five APTS administrators were Asian (Dr. Wonsuk Ma from Korea—academic dean, Dr. Chin Do Kham from Myanmar—dean of students and Dr. Norma Lam from Malaysia—director of the Ministry Development Program). There is no doubt that an Asian will one day serve as president. A beautiful spirit of collegiality has marked the faculty community of the seminary, providing a model for those graduates who will administer Bible school programs throughout the region.

The Annual Lectureship Series

In February 1993, an annual lectureship program to promote Pentecostal theology was begun. Dr. Roger Stronstad, academic dean of Western Pentecostal Bible College, Abbotsford British Columbia, Canada, delivered the first series of lectures. The next year, Dr. Stanley Horton, noted Assemblies of God theologian, was the lecturer, followed by Dr. Walter Kaiser in 1995 and Dr. Russell Spittler in 1996. From the initial year until 2002, Melvin Ho directed this program, which regularly brings to the campus the enrichment of scholars from many parts of the world. These lectures have been videotaped to maximize the value of the experience and provide a means for those not in attendance to benefit from the program. In 1999, the annual lecture series was named the William Menzies Lectureship in honor of Dr. Menzies' distinguished long-term service to the seminary. Table 1 shows the list of lectures conducted through January 2004.

TABLE 1. William Menzies Annual Lectureship Speakers and Topics 1993-2004

YEAR	SPEAKER	TOPIC
1993	Dr. Roger Stronstad	Contemporary Issues in Pentecostal Theology
1994	Dr. Stanley Horton	A Lifetime of Pentecostal Scholarship
1995	Dr. Walter Kaiser Jr.	Continuity and Discontinuity: The Relationship of the Old to the New Testament
1996	Dr. Russell P. Spitler Jr.	Corinthian Spirituality: Cause & Cure
1997	Dr. Andrew F. Walls	Christian History Reconsidered: Towards a Truly Global Church History
1998	Dr. Rikki E. Watts	Jesus and His Mighty Deeds: A Biblical Theological Perspective
1999	Dr. Simon Chan	Pentecostal Reality & the Christian Spiritual Tradition
2000	Dr. Leslie C. Allen	Spirituality in the Psalms
2001	Dr. Delbert Tarr	Spiritual Gifts in Missions Global Contexts
2002	Dr. Paul C. Pierson	The Church in Missions: Changing Contexts and Contemporary Challenges

Year	Speaker	Topic
2003	Dr. Vinay Samuel	Contemporary Challenge to Christian Mission
2004	Dr. Peter Kuzmic	Pentecostalism as a Worldwide Faith in the Maelstrom of Globalization

Beginning in 1997, Dr. Wonsuk Ma organized a second series of lectures, called the Occasional Pentecostal Lectures. These considered a variety of topics related to Pentecostalism but focused especially on the development of the Pentecostal movement in various areas of the world. Table 2 presents a list of the lectures, speakers and topics covered.

TABLE 2. Occasional Pentecostal Lecture Series 1997-2003

YEAR	SPEAKER	TOPIC
February 1997	Dr. Vinson Synan	The Pentecostal and Charismatic Movements in the Twentieth Century
September 1998	Dr. Mathew Clark	The Apostolic Faith Mission of South Africa
February 1999	Dr. Jean-Daniel Pluss	European Pentecostalism
August 2000	Dr. William Kay	British Pentecostalism: An Empirical Perspective
February 2001	Dr. David Daniels	African-American Pentecostalism
March 2001	Dr. William Menzies	Non-Wesleyan Pentecostalism: A Tradition
July 2001	Dr. Frank Macchia	Theological Foundations of Life in the Spirit
October 2001	Dr. A. C. George	Indian Pentecostalism
February 2002	Dr. Peter Hocken	The Holy Spirit and the Renewal of the Catholic Church
July 2002	Dr. David Reed	Oneness Pentecostalism
August 2003	Dr. Deborah Gill	Female Prophets in the Bible Tradition

The APTS Press

Another milestone was reached with the creation of the APTS Press in 1995, which came into being to provide literature for the Pentecostal world, particularly for Asia. The first volume published under this banner was *Spirit, Scripture, and Theology* by Dr. Roger Stronstad, followed in 2001 by *Reflections of an Early American Pentecostal* by Dr. Stanley Horton. In 2003, *The Cross Among Pagodas: A History of the Assemblies of God Myanmar* by Chin Khua Khai was added. *Reflections on Developing Asian Pentecostal Leaders: Essays in Honor of Harold Kohl* by Dr. Kay Fountain (editor), and *Zeal with Knowledge: The First Forty years of FEAST/APTS* by Dr. William Menzies and Dr. John Carter were published in 2004.

Dr. John Carter Becomes President

In July 1995, it became necessary for the Menzies family to return to the USA due to the uncertain health of Doris. Later that year, Dr. William Menzies submitted his resignation as president and, in early 1996, the executive committee of the APTS board invited Dr. John Carter to become the seventh president of APTS. This appointment was approved by the full board during its annual meeting in March 1996 and Dr. Carter was installed as president during the graduation service that was conducted the following day. At the same meeting, the board appointed Dr. Menzies to the honorary position of chancellor and Dr. Wonsuk Ma to the role of academic dean. Dr. Ma assumed this position upon returning from the USA in August 1996, following completion of his doctoral studies at Fuller Seminary. Mirroring a pattern observed with earlier presidents, immediately following his installation, Dr. Carter carried the responsibilities of president, academic dean, business administrator and extension director until others began to arrive to assume these roles. Dr. William Menzies continued to serve as a non-resident faculty member.

The Asian Journal of Pentecostal Studies (AJPS)

A long-standing vision of Dr. Wonsuk Ma was to have APTS sponsor an academic journal to promote the study of Pentecostal theology and practice. In January 1998, the first issue of AJPS appeared, listing Dr. William Menzies as editor and Dr. Wonsuk Ma as associate editor. However, Dr. Menzies readily affirmed that Dr. Ma had carried that burden of bringing this journal to the position of international respect it has earned. Dr. Wonsuk Ma gave further expression to this commitment to Asian scholarship by encouraging AGST to initiate a journal focusing on missiology. Thus, in 1999, the first volume of the *Journal of Asian Mission* (JAM) was published, with Dr. Wonsuk Ma as the editor. In 2002, Dr. Julie Ma assumed responsibilities as editor of this important resource on missionary ministry in Asia.

Expansion of the Academic Program

Over the years, APTS has filled a perceived need to provide academic leadership to the Asia Pacific Pentecostal world. Originally, when FEAST came into being, "advanced" meant a fourth year of biblical education for those who had graduated from the various three-year Bible institutes sponsored by the Assemblies of God in the region. By the late 1970s, more and more of the national Bible schools were offering four-year bachelor's level programs. Consequently, APTS gradually discarded all undergraduate programs and concentrated on offering graduate programs exclusively. This transition was fully completed by the early 1990s.

APTS continued the expansion of the curriculum under the leadership of Dr. Ma in the early 2000s. A post-graduate program leading to a Th.M. degree in Pentecostal/Charismatic Studies was initiated in 2000, graduating the first three students from this program in March 2003: Conrado Lumahan (1985, 1986, 1994), pastor from San Fernando, La Union, Philippines, and district superintendent of the Northern Luzon District Council of PGCAG; Doreen Alcoran, faculty member at the Asian Seminary of Christian Ministries, a Church of God seminary in Manila; and Chang-Soo Kang, a Korean missionary. Although APTS has continued to cooperate with the AGST postgraduate programs, this was the first instance of the seminary offering such a program in its own name.

For a number of years, APTS had sought to provide a way for students to study at the Ph.D. level without leaving Asia. This goal was realized in 2000 when the seminary signed an agreement with the University of Wales, Bangor, in the UK, to offer a "split" Ph.D. program in which students could study at APTS while earning a Wales degree. Following completion of his Th.M. degree in March 2003, Chang-Soo Kang became the first student to enroll in this program.

In 2002, a D.Min. degree program in Pentecostal/Charismatic Ministries was added. Both the Th.M. and D.Min. post-graduate programs represented the continuing emphasis of the seminary on the development of Asian Pentecostalism.

Enhanced Accreditation Standing

ATESEA visited APTS in 1999 for its periodic accreditation review and re-accredited the M.A. and M.Div. programs, removing all of the notations (for deficiencies) noted in the 1991 accreditation visit. Also in 1999, following a comprehensive self-study and visiting team review, APTS was accredited by APTA and, in early 2000, the Asia Theological Association (ATA) visited the school and accredited its programs. Thus, APTS achieved the distinction of being the only seminary accredited by all three of the accrediting agencies offering services in the Asia Pacific region. In 2003, following another periodic review, ATESEA extended the accreditation of APTS to the Th.M. degree program. Because of its outstanding accreditation standing, APTS alumni have been admitted for further study in many theological schools in the USA and Europe.

Developments in the Extension Program

From the early days of FEAST, the leadership envisioned the school taking its resources to the whole region through extension course offerings. As the national Bible schools matured, the extension services of FEAST/APTS changed. The need for undergraduate extension courses diminished and the need for graduate courses offered on-site increased. During the 1990s and early 2000s, the extension program was conducted in Malaysia, Singapore, Indonesia, Fiji, Australia, and the Philippines (Manila, Iloilo, Cebu and Olongapo) and individual courses were offered in Saipan, New Zealand, Mongolia and China. Extension directors during the 1990s included Dr. David Lim, Dr. Jack Rozell, Dr. John Carter (as part of his responsibilities as academic dean) and Donna Brown. In 2001, Dr. Galen Hertweck assumed responsibility for this complex and important service of APTS. Under his leadership, extension sites are being developed in Myanmar and Northern Asia and the number of courses being offered in the extension program has greatly increased.

Construction of the Asia Pacific Center for the Advancement of Leadership and Missions (APCALM)

Soon after assuming office, Dr. Carter began to give attention to the expansion of campus facilities. Following the second phase of construction completed in 1992, the campus provided for a student body of approximately one hundred graduate students, allowing for a fair proportion of these to be married students with families. However, as the decade drew to a close, graduate student enrollment on campus each term was regularly exceeding one hundred, with steady increases expected in subsequent years. (Indeed, during the 2002-2003 academic year, enrollment averaged a record level of 124 students over the three trimesters.) Not only was campus housing approaching saturation in most terms, especially for married students, but there was also a need for additional faculty offices and improved and expanded dining facilities. Moreover, the ability to offer an expanding number of special summer programs such as the MTP and IIS was being limited by the growth in enrollment in the regular graduate programs. A new facility was needed if plans for missions training and other leadership development programs were to proceed.

With the help of Loren Triplett, executive director of the DFM-USA, and the Asia Pacific Field Director, Bob Houlihan, fund raising had been initiated under the tenure of Dr. Menzies to purchase a parcel of land adjacent to the campus, across a deep ravine lying toward the southwest. An offer to purchase had been accepted by the owner and a date to complete the transaction was set for March 1996, giving time for APTS to complete the fund raising. However, the owner, a family-owned corporation, had difficulty clearing the title, which resulted in repeated delays lasting months beyond the agreed date. The purchase had not been finalized when missionary architect David Damron from Springfield, Missouri, visited the campus in October 1996 at the invitation of Dr. Carter to develop initial plans for a facility on the new property. His analysis indicated that the cost to build a facility on the new land, including construction of a bridge across the ravine and new roads to the building site, was much more than had been assumed. Also, since the facility would be at some distance from the main campus, it would require its own utilities, staffing and security arrangements. With this information and given the delay in completing the purchase (constituting a default on the terms of the purchase agreement on the part of the seller), Dr. Carter recommended that the offer to purchase the land be withdrawn and a new site on the lower portion of the main campus be developed for the proposed facility. There were several advantages to the closer site, including both lower costs of construction and the ability to integrate the use of the facility into the overall operation of the campus. This recommendation was approved by the board and the offer to purchase was withdrawn in early 1997.

Over the next two years, Damron, working with design ideas and requirements provided by Dr. Carter, prepared preliminary designs for the new building. At the board meeting in March 1999, with some trepidation, Dr. Carter presented a proposal for the construction of a facility much larger than what had been previously envisioned, and at a much higher projected cost. The size was dictated both by the hillside location of the structure and the anticipation of campus needs over future years. As such, the proposed facility was projected to cost $1.5 million. It was clear, however, that if the facility were to serve the growing needs of the seminary, it would take a structure of these dimensions. After considerable discussion and prayer, the board unanimously approved the project. Later, when an additional floor was added to the front portion of the building, the budget increased to $1.6 million. At the same meeting, the board named the facility the Asia Pacific Center for the Advancement of Leadership and Missions (APCALM) to reflect its primary purpose of providing training for

Asian missionaries, and established APCALM as a department of APTS under the administrative control of the seminary. Immediately following the board meeting, a groundbreaking service was conducted on the construction site, led by Dr. Carter.

APCALM was designed to provide for short-term leadership and missions courses and to host missions and pastors retreats and conferences. A 350-seat chapel, cafeteria adequate to serve over 200 at a sitting, dormitory rooms and apartments to house over 200, as well as faculty offices, conference rooms and apartments for visiting professors were included. It was envisioned that with the completion of APCALM, APTS could conduct multiple short-term special programs on campus without interfering with the regular graduate programs concurrently being conducted.

Board member Ron Maddux, who had served for many years as area director for Peninsular Asia and in 2000 became regional director for Northern Asia, accepted the role of director of development at the outset of the APCALM project, committing himself to raise funds for the endeavor. Working with a group of dedicated missionaries and pastors who caught the vision for the construction of a missions training center on the campus of APTS, $1.6 million was raised for the project over a period of two years while construction was going on. Notably, missionaries Terry Waisner and Bill Prevette, working with the project organized by Maddux, each raised over $100,000 for APCALM, as did Asia Pacific regional director Russ Turney. First Assembly of God, North Little Rock, Arkansas, (Alton Garrison, pastor) and Bethesda Ministries of Colorado Springs, Colorado, each contributed $100,000. Numerous other churches and missionaries made significant donations.

Needing a construction supervisor, Dr. Carter enlisted the services of Huub Luyk, an engineer who had previously directed the construction of an additional floor on Esperanza Hall, remodeling the facility to provide two spacious and attractive faculty apartment units. Luyk, a Dutch Christian who had moved to the Philippines, married a local girl, raised a family, and started a construction business, enthusiastically undertook this responsibility. In March 1999, he assumed direction of the construction of the seven-story, 5200 m^2 (55,000 ft^2) project. At times, more than 250 Filipino workers were involved in the construction. Mark McCormick, an American missionary associate, and Luke Bryant, an engineer, also provided valuable assistance in the construction process during their one-year assignments.

Echoing a similar situation reported by Harold Kohl during the construction of the original FEAST building, in January 2001, funds ran out to continue construction. Several major commitments, totaling more than $100,000, that had been expected during December 2000 had not been included in the January DFM disbursement. With the dedication scheduled for the end of March and many missions leaders making plans to attend, Dr. Carter communicated with Russ Turney, Ron Maddux and others that unless God provided a miracle of financial provision, APTS would have to suspend construction and delay the completion of the building. The campus community was asked to pray and within several days Dr. Carter had an answer. Russ Turney identified $100,000 that could be immediately disbursed, APTS resident missionaries made commitments of $13,000 from their work accounts and several other missionaries communicated their intention to help. With these commitments, and cost cutting efforts by the construction team, the project continued without interruption.

APCALM was dedicated on March 31, 2001, with the keynote address given by John Bueno, executive director of AGWM-USA. Also participating were missions directors and national leaders from several Asian countries, Australia, Canada and the USA. During the dedication service, Ron Maddux raised commitments for the remaining $200,000 needed to complete funding for the project. Significantly, the first major event held in APCALM was the Worldwide Consultation on Cross-Cultural Missions that brought together Assemblies of God missionaries and national missions leaders from around the world. Already the vision that gave birth to APCALM was being realized. In March 2003, a beautiful central courtyard was completed for APCALM and dedicated to the memory of Howard and Edith Osgood, pioneer Assemblies of God missionaries to China from 1929 to 1949. It was fitting that their grandson, Dr. Howard Kenyon, himself a missionary, provided an overview of the ministry of the Osgoods, and a current student from China gave a stirring testimony of what the missionary efforts in China meant to him. Also in attendance on that occasion were the parents of Dr. Howard Kenyon, Gerritt and Anita Kenyon (daughter of Howard and Edith Osgood) and June Hurst, widow of Wesley Hurst, who was so instrumental in the development of the APTS campus in Baguio City in his role as missions director for the Far East during the 1980s. In mid-2003, a gazebo and covered viewing area were added to complete the courtyard development. The courtyard provides both a beautiful and peaceful setting for prayer and meditation.

Campus Expansion and Development

Since the early 1990s, APTS leadership had sought to enlarge the original four-hectare (ten-acre) campus. This lengthy process finally bore fruit in the late 1990s with the purchase of additional parcels of land adjacent to the present campus, comprising approximately 3700 m^2. These acquisitions provide space for the construction of future campus facilities.

Recent developments have included extensive remodeling of Ketcham Hall, previously used as a dining hall and student center, to provide additional space for the library, offices for the registrar and additional faculty offices. In 2003, a 157-year-old octagonal Nipa Hut (originally built in 1846) was transferred to and erected on campus. The octagonal design of this Nipa Hut is unique to Kalinga province and this was the last one of its type remaining there. Since it was to be sold and moved, APTS obtained it for the purpose of cultural preservation. Manny Garcia, a retired Filipino businessman and member of the APTS advisory council, arranged for its transfer and donated funds to cover a portion of the cost. Also in 2003, a cover was constructed over the current basketball court and side bleachers were installed along one side to provide an all-weather recreational facility for basketball, volleyball and tennis. Future development plans include construction of a new library, maintenance building and faculty housing.

Faculty, Missionaries and Staff During the 1990s and Early 2000s

How can one adequately acknowledge all the people who have rendered sacrificial and faithful service to FEAST/APTS over the years? Space does not permit a complete roster. Certainly, some who have rendered conspicuous service will be missed in any recital, but this is not intended. Likewise, we attempted to find photos of faculty and missionaries who served full-time for a year or more, as well as the outstanding students, although some could not be found in the archives.

Dave Oleson came to APTS to serve as business administrator in 1990, following a period as president of Immanuel Bible College in Cebu, serving for three years after the departure of Ken McComber. His wife, Patti, working with Louise Ho, established Christian Academy of Baguio (CAB) where many children of APTS students and faculty have attended. CAB classes were originally held on the APTS campus, but eventually moved to facilities on the campus of the Lutheran Seminary after outgrowing those at APTS. Louise Ho also served as the APTS campus nurse for several years.

New Testament scholar and author, Dr. Robert Menzies, served on the faculty from 1990 to 1993 before he and his family moved to China for ministry. However, he continues to serve as a non-resident faculty member, teaching regularly at the seminary. Others who serve as non-resident faculty include Dr. Paul Lewis, Dr. Timothy P. Jenney, David Hymes and Melvin Johnson. Melvin Ho served on the faculty from 1992 to 2002 and Donna Brown from 1998 to 2002. APTS has been greatly blessed through the years by those willing to share their expertise to train leaders for the region.

Between 1993 and 1998, the position of business administrator was filled for various periods by Nina Colley (2000), Roland Ooi (1993) from Malaysia, Sandy Wilks (1995) and Mike Langford. Keith Kidwell assumed this key role in 1998, holding the position for four years, the longest period since the departure of Ken McComber. Keith and Mary Kidwell served the school with excellence throughout this period, which included the construction of APCALM. Mary led a committee of campus women who were responsible for the interior decoration of the facility. In 2002, John and Eva Kramar came for one year. John, a retired public-school superintendent from the USA, served as business administrator, bringing considerable administrative expertise to the role. In 2003, Dr. Roger Pricer, who had served as a school administrator in the USA and Guam, accepted an assignment to this office. Roger and his wife, Nelda, arrived in June 2003.

Sandy and Melany Wilks both graduated from APTS with high honors and served in the 1990s in various ways. Sandy was administrative assistant, both to Dr. Menzies and Dr. Carter, rendering such varied services as being editor of the *Courier* (the school newsletter), supervising the videotaping of the annual lectureships, helping to develop promotional materials, representing the school at the annual Philippines General Council in Manila, and serving a short stint as acting business administrator. Melany served as library coordinator after Gary Flokstra returned to the USA.

Dr. Joseph Suico from the Philippines became dean of students in 1994, a position he held until 1999 when he and his family moved to England for his Ph.D. studies. Dr. Chin Do Kham from Myanmar (through missionary appointment with AGWM-USA) then served in this role until he and his family returned to the USA in December 2002. His wife, Dr. Siraporn Kham, also served on the faculty. In 2002, Dr. Kay Fountain became associate academic dean for the Center for Asian Pentecostal Studies (CAPS) through which the APTS post-graduate programs (Th.M. and D.Min.) are administered. Eric Lamb served as a computer specialist for two years in the mid-1990s and set up the first LAN system at APTS. Debbie Langley (now Debbie Johnson) was the English instructor for a year in the mid-1990s. Dr. Ruth Peever came to APTS in 2000 after seventeen years in China as an English instructor. She supervises the APTS English as a Second Language program. James Wright served during the 2000-2001 academic year as the biblical language instructor. Recent additions to the faculty include Kaye Cole (2001), who joined the faculty development program in 2002, and Dr. Todd and Heidi LaBute who came in late 2002. Dr. LaBute teaches Systematic Theology. In July 2003, Dr. Joseph Suico resumed the role of dean of students upon his return from England, having completed his Ph.D. That same year, Dr. Jim Davis, who had served as an extension instructor on many occasions through the years and more recently as a visiting professor to the resident campus, accepted the invitation to serve as director of development.

Leota Morar, who had served as a missionary to the Philippines with her husband, John, prior to his death, was APTS registrar from 1995 to 1997. Sheree Moon then filled this position from 1997 to 2003, devoting much effort to developing systems for the office and training staff to carry on following her departure. Stuart German served for two years in the early 1990s as assistant business administrator. Audrey Kum, missionary from Malaysia, worked for two years with the APTS Press in the mid-1990s, preparing many of the seminary's promotional brochures. Her drawing of the upper campus was used in many promotional items, including the APTS mug. Kathy Baxter served as campus nurse from 1998 to 2002, rendering compassionate assistance to many students. Bob and Marilyn Stefan served as missionary associates for several years in the late 1990s and early 2000s. Bob's most important contribution was in preparing a proposal to the Chatlos Foundation that resulted in the first foundation grant in the history of APTS—providing $10,000 for student scholarships in November 2003.

Erlinda (Erl) Reyes (2000), a Filipino missionary, has served APTS in recent years in the promotions and alumni areas. Sam and Stephanie Maddux came in 2003 for a year of service with MDP, and Mayo (2000) and Rhea Catanes (2002), Filipino missionaries, also assisted with the ministries of MDP during 2003.

Nor should we overlook the many faithful Filipino staff members who have served the school through the years. Appendix B lists thirty-one staff members who have served APTS for ten years or more. Their loyalty to the seminary goes well beyond its being a place of employment, but is seen in their commitment to the purposes and ministries of APTS. For instance, many members of the staff are regularly involved on their own time in the ministries of MDP.

Perhaps it is especially appropriate to highlight the service of the APTS staff managers. Ely Sebiano, personnel and business services manager, has served with APTS since May 1987, when she was hired in her early twenties as a cashier. That same month, Joseph Caluza, plant and facilities supervisor, was hired as a member of the maintenance crew. Both Ely and Joseph have distinguished themselves as loyal and effective employees whose promotion to increasing levels of responsibility testifies to their excellent service. Roda Paredes, food services manager, was hired in 1991 to manage a small kitchen in Ketcham Hall. In that crowded facility, she and her staff prepared meals for students and guests that seldom exceeded more than twenty to thirty student diners. However, in 2001, her responsibilities increased dramatically with the move to the APCALM facility. Instead of serving diners numbered in the 20s and 30s, she now routinely feeds groups exceeding several hundred. Roda's ability to adapt to the changing demands of the APTS food service has been a great blessing to the school. Wilma Requina, assistant registrar, first came to APTS in 1987 to serve as the president's secretary. After several years, she moved to Manila to work with AP2000, the Assemblies of God media ministry. She returned to Baguio City and APTS in 1996, following the death of her husband, to serve under Sheree Moon as assistant registrar. When Sheree left unexpectedly in 2002, Wilma assumed responsibility for managing the registrar's office, which she has done with a high degree of efficiency. The newest staff manager is Linda Moises who came to the seminary in 2002 to manage the developing operations of APCALM after having served as the general manager of a resort near Dagupan. Even during her short tenure, her outstanding professionalism and effective management have been instrumental in the development of the ministries and services of the center to a degree not realized before.

We should also mention Glo Royeca, accounting supervisor, who has been acknowledged as the employee of the year on several occasions, and Janet Apolonio, receptionist, whose bright spirit and helpful attitude gives visitors a wonderful first impression of APTS. Finally, Lou Gomez, also a recipient of the employee of the year award, has served as executive secretary and administrative assistant to both Dr. Menzies and Dr. Carter. Her efficient handling of the many tasks of the president's office, including serving as editor of the school newsletter, the *Courier*, has been critical in the effective functioning of the president's office.

Several members of the board of Theological Foundation for Asia (TFA) served for many years, providing a valuable service to the seminary in fulfilling the government requirement for a corporate board with majority membership by Filipino citizens. Among these are Dick Spencer, Virginia Cruz, Elena Castillo, Felipe Acena and Danny Romero.

Outstanding Students of 1990s and Early 2000s

Although they have fewer years of post-APTS service than those coming from earlier periods, the graduates of the 1990s and early 2000s have also distinguished themselves in significant ministries. Among these are Roli dela Cruz, Dr. Norma Lam, and Dr. Kay Fountain who became members of the APTS faculty.

Gatut Budiyono (1990) served for many years as academic dean of Sekolah Tinggi Theologia Satyabhakti (STT-SATI) in Malang, Indonesia, the leading school of the Assemblies of God of Indonesia, and will become the new principal of the school in mid-2004. Emmanuel Fave (1992) became president of Jubilee Bible College in Papua New Guinea and education director for the Assemblies of God of that nation. Zia Paul (1998, 2000), the first student from Pakistan, pastors the largest Assemblies of God church in that country. Keiji Wada (1998, 1999) pastors one of the fastest growing Assemblies of God churches in Japan. Arslan Otgontsetseg (1999) came to APTS as one of the first four students from the newly planted Assemblies of God national church of Mongolia (started in 1993). In 2002, she became the first national leader to serve as chair of the Assemblies of God of Mongolia. David Cartledge (2000), an internationally prominent speaker within the Charismatic and Pentecostal movements, and president for many years of Southern Cross College (formerly Commonwealth Bible College) of the Assemblies of God of Australia, completed an APTS masters degree through the Australia extension along with his wife, Marie (2000). He was the commencement speaker at the time of his own graduation in March 2000, an unusual distinction for a graduating student.

Enrollment Trends in the 1990s and Early 2000s

Enrollment in APTS increased at a steady rate through the decade of the 1990s and early 2000s, reaching an average of 124 students per trimester in the 2002-2003 academic year (the last full year for which statistics are available). This compares to an average of fifty-five students per trimester a decade earlier (1992-1993), an increase of 126 percent over the earlier period.

Enrollment in the extension program averaged ninety-seven over this same period, but varied considerably year by year as a function of the number of operational sites. The highest enrollment for the period was 123 students in 1993-1994, with the second highest enrollment coming in the most recent year (2002) with 110 students. Table 3 shows the average number of students enrolled each year since 1992-93 for both the resident and extension programs and the total enrollment for each year.

TABLE 3. Resident Campus, Extension and Total Enrollment for Period from 1992-2003

ACADEMIC YEAR	RESIDENT CAMPUS ENROLLMENT	CALENDAR YEAR	EXTENSION ENROLLMENT	TOTAL ENROLLMENT
1992-1993	55	1992	112	167
1993-1994	56	1993	123	179
1994-1995	60	1994	81	141
1995-1996	60	1995	81	141
1996-1997	66	1996	102	168
1997-1998	81	1997	94	175
1998-1999	101	1998	98	199
1999-2000	104	1999	99	203
2000-2001	96	2000	94	190
2001-2002	94	2001	76	170
2002-2003	124	2002	110	234

A New President to Begin the Fifth Decade

In July 2002, Dr. John Carter gave notice to the board that he did not wish to be considered for a new five-year term as president when his current term ended in March 2004. Following a policy adopted by the board several years earlier, the executive committee named a presidential search committee to identify potential candidates, especially Asian candidates. The committee included several members of the board, an APTS administrator, and an APTS alumnus serving as pastor. Although it was expected that it might be possible to name an Asian president at this time, none of the several Asian nominees agreed to be considered. Consequently, at its meeting in March 2003, the board named Dr. Wayne Cagle president-elect to take office in April 2004. Dr. Cagle is a veteran Asia Pacific missionary who served in

Indonesia and as area director for Pacific Oceania from 1986 to 2003. Dr. Cagle and his wife, Dr. Judy Cagle, both completed D.Min. degrees at the Assemblies of God Theological Seminary (AGTS) in Springfield, Missouri, in 2002. Their rich background of ministry in the region will be a blessing in their leadership of the seminary.

Into the New Millennium

It is now more than forty years since the vision of Maynard Ketcham was first articulated. Over the years, many individuals and church bodies have shared in the fulfillment of the dream of providing quality leadership training for the Pentecostal churches of the Asia Pacific region. Without a doubt, APTS has served a significant role in facilitating the growth of Bible schools and institutes in many lands. Many of the administrators and faculty members of the Bible schools of the region have been mentored at APTS. A large number of national church leaders, pastors, evangelists and missionaries throughout East Asia and the Pacific Islands are alumni. APTS has proven to be a bastion of theological stability, spiritual fervor, and evangelistic and missionary vision. The motto emblazoned on the stained-glass window adorning the southwest wall of Hurst Hall continues to give focus to the mission of the school: Zeal with Knowledge.

As the new APCALM facility has begun to be used, an exciting new chapter in the history of APTS is beginning to unfold. National churches that just a generation or so ago were "receiving" nations are now taking their place alongside older Western church bodies as "sending" churches. Picture teams of zealous workers coming from local churches and the schools of many lands, eager for intensive cross-cultural training in missions. An army of Spirit-filled workers is on the way! There remains a vast harvest field to be reached—nearly half of the world's population. Let us pray for one another that we may together bear strong witness to the love of Christ for a lost world. This is the heart of the mission of APTS in this new millennium.

Zeal with Knowledge
The First Sixty Years of FEAST/APTS
Photo Gallery 2

Hurst Hall & Sign

Staff (1st Year in Baguio City)

Dr. Klaude Kendrick

President David Lim

AdCom 1989

Dr. William Menzies

Dr. Joseph Suico teaching in the mid-1990s

Bethesda Construction 1990

Collapse of Hyatt Hotel

Students after the earthquake

MDP Medical Outreach

Gary Flokstra leading a library seminar

John & Bea Carter in 1991

MTP Students 1998

Dr. Roger Stronstad

Faculty 1996

APCALM Construction

APCALM Dedication with
Dr. John Carter leading

Osgood Courtyard 2003

APTS Admin Comm 1991

Faculty & Spouses 1992

TFA 2000

Graduates 1999

Graduates 2003

Board 2003

Dr. Wayne Cagle

Hal and Bea Kohl 2003

APCALM Building

A New Season: (2004-2014)
Dr. Wayne Cagle Becomes President

The fortieth-anniversary celebration also saw the inauguration of a new president, Dr. Wayne Cagle, selected after several Asians removed their names from consideration. The departing president, Dr. John Carter, continued for two more years as a regular faculty member before moving to Australia for a special assignment. He remained as an adjunct instructor at APTS and returned to campus several times to teach and later served as chairman of the board. When he stepped down from the board in 2016, APTS honored him and Bea for their twenty-five years of service with a festschrift entitled, *Theological Education in a Cross-Cultural Context: Essays in Honor of John and Bea Carter*, edited by long-time colleague Dr. Kay Fountain. In 2006, he was honored with the title of president emeritus.

As he prepared to depart from his office, Dr. Carter noted that the school had nearly nine hundred alumni serving all over Asia and other parts of the world, a number of them in significant leadership positions. By 2004, enrollment stood at an average of ninety-eight students, with another 139 enrolled in the extension programs throughout the region. The enrollment together with successful summer programs led Dr. Carter to remark that APTS was truly making an impact on the region. While APTS was largely achieving its mission, he also said that the school must rise to meet the demands of the present rather than rest on past victories. The aggressive church planting by the Assemblies of God churches in the region would call for increased numbers of Bible schools that would require APTS to train more faculty. He also concluded that the rising number of missionaries from the Asia Pacific nations and Pacific Oceana places a burden on APTS for theological and missiological training.

Drs. Wayne and Judy Cagle were not new to APTS. Wayne had attended FEAST as a student, both on the main campus and the extension campus in Indonesia while serving there. He also taught an APTS onsite class in Thailand. This background, along with the Cagles Assemblies of God World Missions USA (AGWM) leadership responsibilities, meant that they already had a long-term relationship with APTS and understood well the school's nature, mission and goals. But having assumed the president's role at the age of sixty-two, they felt from the beginning that they could only commit to one five-year term. After completing their term and after Dr. William Menzies resigned as chancellor, Dr. Cagle became the chancellor and raised funds for APTS in the United States until they retired from AGWM in 2013. He also continued as an AGWM Area Director at large for leadership and training while president of APTS, but turned over the leadership responsibilities in Pacific Oceania to another missionary.

In assuming the presidency, Dr. Cagle stated that his goal was to empower and release the APTS leadership team to execute their areas of responsibility. He established five clear goals for his administration: (1) to double the resident and extension enrollment, (2) to expand facilities with the purchase of new land to add more faculty housing, build a new library/research center, and refurbish an existing building as a health and wellness center, (3) to enhance the successful Asia Pacific Center for the Advancement of Leadership and Missions (APCALM, now GMC) programs with the addition of a new missionary training program, university internship program, unreached people group program and a community action development program and, (4), remain on the cutting edge of scholarship by the development of online programs and the development of Asian faculty through the Faculty Development Program. As is often the case, not all of these goals would be met, but they did represent a compass heading for guiding the school in this period. By the time he left office in 2009, two duplex buildings for faculty housing were built on new land, a five-story Academic Research Center building was erected with space for faculty and administrative offices, a student center, and a library. In addition, the number of alumni would be nearly 1,200.

Another of Dr. Cagle's goals was to raise endowment funds to help reduce the financial load of the president and Asian faculty members, although raising funds for the impending construction projects would have to be his priority. In 2008, the board approved a chair of Intercultural Studies, which was ultimately named after L. John Bueno, the executive director of AGWM from 1997-2012. By 2011, the school had raised about four million dollars for campus development, but funding for faculty endowments was lagging. In 2013, Dr. Teresa Chai, a missionary from Malaysia, became the first and, as of this writing, the only faculty member to occupy this chair. Dr. Cagle also raised a president's endowment fund with an initial endowment grant of $100,000 with a goal of $250,000 for a perpetual endowment to help if the day came when a president from a lesser-resourced country was appointed.

Academics

By this time, the number of programs offered had grown to eight:
- M.A. Ministry
- M.A. Theology
- M.A. Intercultural Studies
- M.A. Intercultural Studies—Islamic Concentration
- M.Div.
- Th.M. in Pentecostal/Charismatic Studies
- D.Min. in Pentecostal/Charismatic Studies
- Ph.D. (in cooperation with the University of Wales in the UK)

Post-Graduate Programs

In the past, the school has provided training particularly for Bible school/college teachers. However, as many schools have begun, or plan to offer master's level education, APTS now needed to provide upgraded training for Bible school teachers and others. This was consistent with APTS' track record of being in the vanguard of Pentecostal theological education in the Asia Pacific region.

As there was no higher theological program in the region specifically designed to train Pentecostals, the school initiated a Th.M. program. By this time, there were sufficient resident regular faculty to handle this program (eight with a Ph.D. and three more completing doctoral studies soon) and it was supplemented by visiting lecturers from the West and Asia. This also provided the APTS faculty the opportunity to engage in more serious levels of academic activity. The first two cohorts were quite successful and produced some quality graduates. In 2005, however, the program was changed to an M.Th. to follow the British system of education more closely. A 2004 Th.M. student questionnaire revealed overwhelming satisfaction in a program that was meeting their needs and answering issues from the students' ministry contexts.

The split-Ph.D. program with the University of Wales, Bangor (UWB), UK, began in 2000. At this point, APTS was not yet in a position to offer its own Ph.D., and association with a well-respected school in Europe would also enhance the prestige of APTS. This was a research-only degree with two supervisors per dissertation, one from each school. The long-term goal, however, was to establish a separate Ph.D. program at APTS. Unfortunately, the UWB phased out of the program in 2009 resulting in only one APTS student, Saw Tint Sann Oo from Myanmar, receiving his Ph.D. this way.

The Extension Program

The extension program continued to be offered in various places around the region. As the AG Bible schools in some countries began to offer their own master's programs, the APTS extension sites moved elsewhere. In 2010, there were extension sites in Myanmar, Thailand, Fiji, Northern Asia, Central Luzon, and Manila in the Philippines, with more being considered. By policy, at least fifty percent of the classes were taught by regular APTS faculty members, the rest were taught by adjuncts. In 2011, after a decade of faithful service in overseeing this ministry, Dr. Galen Hertweck stepped down and was replaced by Dr. Tom Bohnert.

William W. Menzies Annual Lectureship

The Menzies Lectureship continued to be a strong component of the academic program, featuring mainly speakers from the West, including Drs. Judith Lingenfelter, 2005; Allan Anderson, 2006; Amos Yong, 2007; Benny Aker, 2008; Craig Keener, 2009; I. Howard Marshall, 2010; Keith Warrington, 2011; Bob Menzies and Glen Menzies, 2012; Doug Petersen, 2013; and Tim Bulkeley in 2014. A number of their lectures were subsequently published in the *Asian Journal of Pentecostal Studies*. Three time slots were normally allocated at the Lectureship to faculty members, postgraduate students and others to present papers.

Publishing

In continuation of William Menzies' vision for theological reflection, in 2004, in addition to those mentioned earlier, the APTS Press also published *The Church in China: Persecuted, Pentecostal and Powerful*, by Luke Wesley and *David Yonggi Cho: A Close Look at His Theology and Ministry*, edited by Dr. Wonsuk Ma, Dr. William W. Menzies, and Hyeon-sung Bae. This was published in cooperation with Hansei University in Korea. In 2005, a new book, published in cooperation with Regnum International, was titled, *Asian and Pentecostal: The Charismatic Face of Christianity in Asia*, edited by Dr. Allan Anderson and Dr. Edmund Tang; and in 2006, *Pentecost Unto the Uttermost: The History of the Assemblies of God in Samoa*, by Dr. Tavita Pagaialii, was published. Later in this time period the Press published *Theology in Context: A Case Study in the Philippines*, by Dave Johnson, and *Leave a Legacy: Increasing Missionary Longevity*, by Russ Turney.

The APTS journal, the *Asian Journal of Pentecostal Studies*, begun in 1998, continued to be faithfully produced twice a year. By this time, it was gaining an excellent reputation as the flagship publication on Asian Pentecostal studies, which continues to this day. Not only did the publishing give the faculty and others an outlet for their publishing efforts, it also served to expand the awareness of APTS itself.

Registrar's Office

The registrar was tasked with overseeing the admissions and academic records department of the school. The following are the campus and extension enrollment records.

TABLE 4.

RESIDENT CAMPUS		EXTENSION		TOTAL
Academic Year	Enrollment	Calendar Year	Enrollment	Enrollment
2004-2005	267	2004	133	400
2005-2006	199	2005	86	285
2006-2007	145	2006	79	224
2007-2008	131	2007	107	238
2008-2009	137	2008	98	235
2009-2010	123	2009	6	189
2010-2011	125	2010	57	182
2011-2012	124	2011	33	157
2012-2013	112	2012	55	167
2013-2014	102	2013	54	156

Faculty

APTS is different from other schools in two ways. One of those is that the faculty is not ranked, although APTS does seek to promote Asian faculty members to various leadership positions. The purpose is to promote equality in the work of the Lord and in accomplishing the goals of the school. It also gives each faculty member an equal voice in the affairs that affect them. The other way APTS differs from other schools is that missionaries must raise funds for their own salaries, etc. The advantage, apart from enabling the school to survive financially, is that those who teach at APTS really want to be there. Among the many disadvantages, however, is that much time is lost to APTS when faculty members have to return home for extended periods to raise the needed funds.

The normal faculty workload is teaching eighteen credits per school year plus various committee or ministry assignments and possibly summer classes. They are also expected to teach at the various extension sites and pursue some ministry off campus as their schedule permits. The purpose of off-campus ministry is to be a blessing to local congregations as well as keep faculty in touch with what is going in the local churches, which will inform their teaching. The addition of more faculty offices in the new Academic Research Center in 2008 gave the students more access to the faculty and the faculty to each other since many offices were now under one roof instead of being scattered all over campus or in homes. This also enhanced faculty collegiality.

Faculty members are given a lot of freedom to develop and teach their courses in the way that seems best to them within the theological framework of the Assemblies of God's Statement of Fundamental Truths, which all resident faculty members are required to reaffirm annually. Within that framework, debate, discussion, and disagreement, done in the right spirit, is encouraged. This "freedom within a framework" also extends to their publications, where faculty members are encouraged to research and write on themes of interest to them, normally subjects within their field of expertise. They are also encouraged to publish their work in articles and books, and give papers at various symposia around the Asia Pacific region. APTS has endeavored through the years to provide a conducive environment for academic and scholarly activities, including academic freedom. Faculty members are also required to pursue further education if they do not yet have their terminal degrees.

Faculty Transitions (2004-2014)

Continuing Service Throughout This Period

Dr. Kay Fountain continued teaching in the Old Testament and handling various other duties, including the academic dean's role starting in 2012. She was the first female in the history of APTS to serve in this position. Dr. Galen and Dickie Hertweck continued their service to APTS throughout this entire period. Dr. Galen taught Hermeneutics and New Testament courses. He also directed the extension program until 2011 and directed the field education program. Dickie taught in the English Language Program (ELP) and helped students with their term papers. She also served briefly as the library coordinator in 2009 and as the Voluntary Citizens' Liaison of the U.S. Embassy for APTS. Hirokatsu and Miyuke Yoshihara also continued to serve, teaching English and as well as in the missionary training programs.

Departures

In 2006, Drs. Wonsuk and Julie Ma completed their long, outstanding tenure at APTS for him to assume the role of the executive director of the Oxford Center for Missions Studies in the United Kingdom, where Julie became a research mentor. Dr. Wonsuk Ma's twenty-four years of service is the longest faculty tenure in APTS history. Jim and Genevieve Davis and Harold and Kaye Cole also concluded their time at APTS in 2006. Kaye had previously earned her D.Min. and joined the faculty in their later years. Dr. Ruth Peever resigned from the full-time faculty in 2006, but remained on campus in a part-time capacity until 2020, while also pursuing another ministry. In 2007, Mung Lian Sian departed for Ph.D. studies in the States and Todd and Heidi LaBute departed in 2008.

In 2011, Drs. Lem and Rose Engcoy left APTS to pursue other ministries. He taught Pastoral Counseling and she taught Church History as well as heading up the APRC from 2005-11. She continued as an adjunct instructor for several years after they departed. In 2012, Dr. Joseph and Lulu Suico left APTS to pastor a church in Mindanao. Dr. Roli dela Cruz and his wife, Amy, whom he had married in 2006, departed about the same time. Amy, who served as the registrar while here, was an American and they departed to teach in the United States. However, they are now appointed missionaries with AGWM and are preparing to return as of this writing.

Arrivals

In addition to her role as the president's wife, Dr. Judy Cagle also served as a member of the faculty, teaching leadership and Christian education and discipleship courses, as well as overseeing the D.Min. program. Tom and Connie Bohnert and their family arrived in 2004 as AGWM missionaries. Tom taught missions courses and eventually took over the summer programs and student ministries. He received his D.Min. from the Assemblies of God Theological Seminary in Springfield, Missouri, in 2006. He also replaced Galen Hertweck as director of the extension program in 2011, as well as serving in other capacities.

Tham Wan Yee and his wife, Moon Tee Ngoh, and their family were sent out by the Malaysian Assemblies of God and Tham Wan joined the faculty when he arrived in 2004. An APTS M.Div. graduate, Tham Wan would eventually get his Th.M. through the Faculty Development Program. He succeeded Dr. Jim Davis as the director for seminary advancement in 2006 and would succeed Dr. Wayne Cagle as president in 2009.

Steve and Ella Carter served from 2004-05. Steve taught Research Methods and Pentecostalism and served as registrar and library coordinator. AGWM missionaries David and Anna Hymes came from Japan to serve at APTS from 2005-09. David had an M.Th. and taught Old Testament, Hebrew and Research Methods and Anna served as the library coordinator. They returned to Japan in 2009. AGWM missionaries Dr. Chris and Lindsey Carter arrived in 2005. Chris taught New Testament, Biblical Languages, and Hermeneutics. They transferred to Japan in 2009. Rueben Ovsepyan, from Russia, an APTS alumnus, taught Research Methods from 2006-07.

Dr. Paul Lewis arrived on campus in 2006 with his wife, Eveline, who was originally from Indonesia, and their two daughters. The Lewises had served for a number of years as AGWM missionaries in China and had also been serving as non-resident regular faculty members of APTS since 1997, teaching one trimester a year on campus. He succeeded Dr. Wonsuk Ma as the academic dean and Eveline served in various capacities in the business office, bookstore, and ELP. They returned to the United States in 2012. Americans David and Anetha Beard served a brief stint, with David as the registrar in 2007.

Sam Bowdoin and his wife, Shellie, and their children arrived in 2008 and served in a full-time capacity until 2011. Sam taught Intercultural Studies while also overseeing the GMC programs, including missionary training and Impact Ministries, while completing his Ph.D. in Intercultural Studies at Biola University in Southern

California. Jun Kim, along with his wife, Jane, and family began serving on the faculty in 2009, after completing his M.Div. at APTS. He taught Healing Theology, Systematic Theology, Biblical Hebrew and World Church History.

Nick Wilson, a professional librarian, served as the head librarian from 2010 until his untimely death from cancer in 2016. Due to his illness, he and his wife, Ruth, spent much of their time directing the library from the United States, where he was being treated. Marlene Yap, a Filipino missionary who had previously served in China, joined the faculty in 2010 and taught Greek.

Im Seok (David) Kang came to APTS in 2011 with his wife, Jin Yeong and their two sons. He taught Hebrew and Old Testament. Dr. Joel Tejedo also joined the faculty in 2011, bringing his wife, Carolyn, and their three children. He taught Research Methods, Pentecostalism, and other ministry subjects. He also served in other capacities.

Dr. Joe Liu and his wife, Lana, missionaries from Taiwan, also arrived in 2011 and taught in the Chinese department. June LeBret, a veteran AGWM missionary to the Philippines, joined APTS in 2012 and taught Research Methods until retirement in early 2014, although she continues to teach part-time online until the present. Drs. Weldyn and Barbara Houger joined the APTS family in 2013. He taught missions courses, chaired the Postgraduate Committee, and served two years as the dean of students. Barbara taught Christian Education courses and served as the coordinator for the D.Min. program.

Dr. Dave and Debbie Johnson, also veteran missionaries to the Philippines with AGWM, joined the resident faculty in 2013, seventeen years after they had met on campus while Debbie was teaching English in 1996-97. She took over the helm of the ELP and edited for the APTS Press and the Journal. Dave handled the Journal and the APTS Press, while also serving as the coordinator of the M.Th. program and taught some in the missions program.

Dr. Teresa Chai arrived just a couple of weeks after the Johnsons under appointment with the Malaysian AG and taught missions. Herman Dionson, a Filipino APTS graduate taught briefly as part of the Faculty Development Program from 2013-15. Kent Parrish and his wife joined the team in 2013, with Kent as the registrar and then business administrator. Drs. Richard and Joy Varnell arrived in 2013.

Richard became the director of development in 2014 and Joy taught in the ELP and became an editor for the APTS Press.

Non-resident regular faculty members were those who were not regular faculty but came every year to teach one or two courses. Adjunct faculty members continued to fill in the gaps with courses that the resident or non-resident regular faculty members did not have expertise in or could not do without becoming overloaded. Before the COVID-19 pandemic in 2020, these courses were normally taught in block sessions on campus, with the instructor coming for a 2-3 week stint. While this offered all the advantages mentioned, it also wreaked havoc with the regular classes since the blocks required either all morning or afternoon of the students' time. This meant that blocks often had to be taught on Mondays and even Saturdays when regular classes were not in session.

Faculty Development Program

Since its inception in 1985, The Faculty Development Program has played a significant role in developing Asian faculty members for APTS by helping them attain their post-graduate degrees. Three faculty members completed their degrees during this time. Lian Sian Mung, from Myanmar, completed his M.Th. from APTS in Pentecostal/Charismatic Studies in 2007. Filipino Lemuel Engcoy completed his Ed.D. in Counseling through the AGST in 2008 and his wife, Rose, completed her Ph.D. in Church History in 2013, also through the AGST. Several others began their studies during this time.

Library

The library continued to make excellent progress in getting the 55,000 books (not counting other resources) loaded into the new Alexandria database, which was installed in 2003. The library also provided students with access to computers for online activities and doing their term papers. Four OPAC computer terminals were installed to give users access to the Alexandria system which was controlled by a reservation system. In 2004, the Asia Theological Association considered the APTS library as one of the two top libraries of all the 168 schools that were members of the Association.

Over the years a number of enhancements were also added including the EBSCO 2.0 program. This gave faculty and students access to articles in philosophy and religion, including nearly 300 full-text journals and over 250 peer-reviewed titles, over 47,000 articles and book abstracts in New Testament studies and ATLA serials online databases, including a religion database with over 555,000 article citations and much more.

Asia Pacific Research Center (APRC)

The APRC, under the leadership of faculty member, Dr. Rose Engcoy, flourished during this period. Engcoy focused not only on collecting original materials but also on doing oral interviews with Pentecostal pioneers in the Philippines. To this end, the APRC also partnered with Dr. Dave Johnson, who was writing a book on the history of the AGWM missionaries in the Philippines, by providing transcription services for his oral interviews of Filipinos and former missionaries, in exchange for copies of the interviews for the APRC archives. After the book was published in 2009, he donated copies of most of his research, much of it primary data, to the APRC.

Field Education

All M.Div. students were required to complete a field education program in a ministry of their choice for three months, or 400 hours. This was designed to enhance the development of practical ministry skills. Many of the students accomplished their field education in local churches in the metro Baguio City area, but efforts were also made to do it in other places in Asia as well. This also served to enhance the relationship between the churches and APTS.

Outstanding Students from (2004-2013)

The following students distinguished themselves academically, ministerially and in personal growth and maturity during this time. In the M.A. program they were Suphat Phattanaviroj (Thailand), Glenzer Fernandez (Philippines), Rhea Esphyr Catanes (Philippines), Sohn You Kil (Korea), Edgar Salcedo (Philippines), Jay Angeles (Philippines), Glenn Cruz (Philippines), Shellie Bowdoin (USA), Sophin Smith (Cambodia) and Zaldy Lim (Philippines).

The awardees in the M.Div. program were Lian Sian Mung (Myanmar), Dennis Kurt Covert (Fiji Islands), Denise Ross (Ireland), Amar Pandey (Nepal), Jun Kim (Korea), Roger Dutcher (USA), Su Yan Zong (China), Taehyun Lee (Korea) and Herman Dionson (Philippines). Mesake Sivoinavatu (Fiji Islands) received the award in both categories.

Other Missionaries on Campus (2004-2013)

A school like APTS always has a number of non-faculty positions that need to be filled and many, normally short-termers, served in these positions. In 2004, Filipino missionary Erlinda (Erl) Reyes concluded her service in the alumni department and left to pastor a church in the area. In 2005, Anita Swartz concluded her service to APTS as did Adeline Ladera. Both had served in the Ministry Development Program (MDP) and Adeline had taught briefly in 2013, after finishing her D.Min. at APTS.

Herschel and Judy Gilliland (Kaye Cole's parents) served in the MDP from 2004-05. Bruce and Connie Dawson served from 2005-08 in a variety of capacities, including Bruce serving as the housing coordinator and assistant business administrator and Connie as the alumni office coordinator in 2005, as well as studying. Jonathan and Shannon Belgarde and Jayesun and Michelle Sherman served on campus from 2007-08 while also studying. Both men helped in the MDP and taught in the ELP. Nina Colley Henry, with her husband, Jerry, returned for a brief stint as the business administrator from 2007-08. LaCrisha Pollard taught in the ELP from 2008-09 while teaching at the Christian Academy of Baguio, as did Glenda Dutcher.

Fa Chi (Andrew) Mo and his wife, Alice Huang, were Taiwanese missionaries that joined the campus family in 2009. He worked in the IT office while also studying. Noel and Anna Manayon, a Filipino couple served from 2010-11, in media and seminary promotion. In

Jae Lee and his wife, Kihyang Kim came and he served as the business administrator from 2009-2011. Glenn Machlan taught English in 2010. Heather Jacob (AGWM) served as the business administrator from 2012-14. Sunil Kwoun and his wife, Ham Jong Gum, came from Korea in 2013 and he served as head of the groundskeeping department.

Campus Life

APTS is not focused only on academics, but also on spiritual formation and living together in a multi-cultural community. While the duty of safeguarding the spiritual heritage and Pentecostal distinctives of the Assemblies of God lies with all who serve at APTS, the one primarily overseeing the day-to-day activities related to spiritual formation and the community is the dean of students.

APTS community gatherings for spiritual purposes are dynamic. Chapel services continued three times a week, as did the annual spiritual emphasis week in the first trimester, the missions convention in the second and the Menzies lectureship in the third, providing a balance of head knowledge and heart experiences with God. Opportunities for the moving of the Holy Spirit were given. Although some students came to APTS having not previously experienced the Baptism of the Holy Spirit with the evidence of speaking in other tongues, few left without this experience. There was a conscious effort throughout the seminary, including classroom study, prayer groups and the Annual Lectureship to emphasize the work of the Holy Spirit in the life and ministry of the students. Pentecostal praying was evident in the prayer rooms and corporate prayer sessions, which students find valuable.

Every year, the students elect a student council that is designed to create and oversee students' activities and other responsibilities assigned by the dean of students. These activities included working with the GMC director to host International Night during the annual missions convention, the annual all-school outing and occasional sports fests. They also served as the voice of the students to the administration and students were encouraged to channel their concerns through them.

The dean of students' office was also responsible for the development of the school's yearbook, the *Chalice*. In nearly every case, the effort was led by a selected team of students who donated a lot of hours to the project annually. A special edition was published in time for the Jubilee celebration in 2014.

Due to the multi-cultural environment in APTS with students and faculty coming from twenty or more nations, cultural issues were a significant concern. This cross-cultural mix, while enriching in many ways, also presented challenges as these issues were addressed among students and faculty. Small group settings, and private and classroom discussions were opportunities where specific concerns could be addressed. Students often point to the cross-cultural character of the APTS community as one of the factors that have enhanced their educational experience.

Business Office and Staff Operations

The number of full-time Filipino staff members who served in various functions during this time period fluctuated between fifty-three and thirty-five people, serving in various departments: maintenance, landscaping, food service, housing and guest services, the bookstore, the library and office staff, etc., and were augmented by a number of occasional employees that were called upon when needed. Most of them served under the business administrator and made invaluable contributions to the success of the school.

After the ARC was completed in 2008, the old library in the Hurst building was turned into a Chinese/Korean library and became the new home for the APRC. Two side rooms were converted into study rooms for postgraduate students and another was converted into a storage room for APTS Press. The old building used for MDP and the APRC, which already had a house attached, was converted into a faculty duplex.

Campus Development

Campus development would be a major focus during Dr. Cagle's tenure. By 2005, a total of 5,069 square meters of land was acquired on the south side of the campus for building additional missionary-faculty housing and a Prayer Mountain. Builders International, an

AGWM ministry based in Springfield, Missouri, was also involved in the project. The Asia Pacific Board of Regents helped with $75,000. The Northern California/Nevada District of the AG USA Women's Ministries pledged $60,000, and a generous gift of $240,000 was received from a group called ACTIONOW, headed by American AG minister Tom Paino for the construction of two duplexes. The total project including the land acquisition, infrastructure, site development (retaining walls due to building on the side of hills), and two 2-unit duplexes cost $595,190.92. Each duplex was two stories with a total of 509 sq. meters per duplex. Also in 2006, another 11,741 square meters of land, downhill from the Prayer Mountain and duplexes, in the southeast corner of the campus was purchased for future development. The AG USA's Speed-The-Light donated much equipment including a bulldozer, backhoe, and trucks to assist in construction.

The APCALM facility was three years old but still needed some internal furbishing, including adding new faculty offices, which were completed during this time. A new, larger generator was also installed to provide electricity to APCALM, Bethesda, Sampaguita, and Esperanza whenever there was a brownout in Baguio City.

In 2007, construction was begun on a new building called the Academic Research Center that would contain more classrooms, faculty and administrative offices, a student center and a much larger library with a capacity targeted for 100,000 volumes. It was constructed right next to the Hurst building and the two would, in effect, become one building. To do this, the old Ketcham building, which had served its purpose well, had to be demolished. The five-story, 2,626 square meter Academic Research Center was dedicated on July 2008. The ARC was partially funded through the generosity and partnership of ACTIONOW and PRIORITY ONE led by Sam Johnson. The final bill came to $1,511,604.04.

By 2010, the campus had expanded to 55,731 square meters (5.5 hectares), containing a total of around twenty-four buildings and homes, a multi-purpose sports complex, children's playgrounds and picnic areas. The value of the campus was estimated at between ten and thirty million U.S. dollars.

The Internet

As the school moved deeper into the Information Age, it became apparent that APTS' WIFI access and online presence, or lack thereof, needed to be addressed. By 2006, the APTS website was updated and improved. Finetuning site content and policies had to be developed as time went along. Modular Object-Oriented Dynamic Learning Environment (MOODLE), an online educational platform, was added to help with academics.

Providing WIFI access around the campus has always been a difficult issue to accomplish, in part because of the school's somewhat isolated location a few kilometers outside of downtown Baguio City. Only one internet service provider even had a trunk line running out down Ambuklao Rd that the school could use. Nevertheless, several hotspots were established in various locations on campus.

APCALM Programs/Global Missions Center (GMC)

The APCALM/GMC programs are broadly described as adjunct programs that run during the school year and the summer institutes that are held during the summer break. Some of the summer institutes were annual, others not as often. In 2006, with the departure of Harold Cole and the appointment of Dr. Tom Bohnert as his successor, the ADCOM felt the need to refocus the MDP in other directions. The ADCOM merged the ministries of the MDP and APCALM under one umbrella and renamed both programs and the building itself as the Global Missions Center and the MDP was renamed as Impact Ministries.

Programs During the School Year

Ministry Development Program

Students continued to be encouraged to engage in various ministries, both through the MDP program and in other avenues. The Ministry Development Program included medical outreaches, prison ministry, elementary school ministry, and others. Students also got involved in local churches, especially those that had English services. By 2004, the literature distribution program had served nearly seven hundred churches in Northern Luzon each quarter. In 2006, with the restructuring of the MDP and APCALM ministries, the costly literature distribution program, as valuable as it had been, was discontinued and donors were requested to redirect their support to other ministries within the GMC.

The English Language Program (ELP)

The ELP continued to help students improve their English so that they could succeed in their degree programs. Some even started the program with no proficiency in English at all. When Dr. Ruth Peever, who had served as the director for many years resigned, Lawrence and Melanie Tucker, missionaries with the Summer Institute of Linguistics (SIL) took over the program under a special arrangement with APTS.

In 2013, Debbie Johnson assumed the leadership of the program when the Tuckers left and introduced some innovations designed to help students focus more on the theological words and concepts they would need to know in their studies. One of the changes allowed students to sit in regular classes with a cooperating faculty member to listen to the English and then retire to the English classroom to review the vocabulary and grammar used in the regular class. Another innovation allowed upper-level English students to slowly begin taking regular classes, perhaps one or two a trimester while finishing the English program rather than finishing the English program first and then diving into a full regular class schedule. This allowed the students to proceed more slowly to absorb theological English more firmly. Having had to learn two languages as an adult herself, Russian and Tagalog, as well as having a master's degree in Teaching English to Speakers of Other Languages (TESOL), she well understood the students' situation and how to help them.

The Annual Missions Convention

Held during the second trimester of the school year, the missions convention is designed to challenge students to see beyond their communities and embrace the reality that many of the world's 7,400 Unreached People Groups, with a total population of about three billion people, live in Asia and have little to no access to the gospel. Students are challenged to go as missionaries, pray and give to missions efforts while they are at APTS and after they have graduated. Several thousand dollars are raised annually. Once the missions pledges have been made, the student council selects which projects will be supported for the coming year. One of the highlights of the year is the International Night on the last evening of the convention, where students prepare and share foods from their homelands. They also dress in their national costumes and participate in an evening program featuring cultural skits, songs, and other presentations representing their homelands.

Summer Institutes

At this time, the summer institutes, most geared toward practical ministries, included the Institute for Islamic Studies (IIS), Institute for Buddhist Studies (IBS), the Missionary Training Program, and the Leadership Development Institute that the Cagles had inaugurated before becoming president and continued to lead themselves. This was the focus of Dr. Wayne Cagle's D.Min. dissertation. Other new institutes were being contemplated and planned.

The Missionary Training Program was designed to prepare men and women for missionary work in a cross-cultural setting. The focus here is on developing competent missionary skills. The Institute for Islamic Studies does the same, with the addition that times of personal devotion and intercessory prayer are built into the curriculum. This program came into acute focus after the destruction of the World Trade Centers in New York City on September 11, 2001. Both courses could be taken for credit at the graduate and undergraduate levels. The APCALM/GMC summer programs were closely connected to ministries such as the Assemblies of God Asian Mission Association (AGAMA), Center for Ministry to Muslims (now Global Initiative), and others, demonstrating APTS' high-level commitment and ability to network with others. After AGAMA was shut down, the missionary program was reorganized and restarted as the Missionary Training Institute (MTI).

The Leadership Development Institute (LDI) had four core modules entitled: (1) The Biblical Leader, (2) The Biblical Leader Develops and Communicates a Vision, (3) The Assessment of the Biblical Leader, and (4) Being an Excellent Leader. Other modules were added later for a second LDI. These modules were entitled: (1) Conflict Management, (2) Strategic Planning, and (3) Power and Leadership and Mentoring. General Council leaders, pastors and missionaries came from Asia Pacific nations for several weeks for concentrated studies in the APCALM building on campus.

A program for reaching Buddhists, called the Institute for Buddhist Studies, was also held for several years under the leadership of Thailand AGWM missionary Dr. Alan Johnson, to train workers for the Buddhist world. In addition, the Asian Institute in Youth Studies (AIYS), long a staple GMC program, continued to host institutes on campus as did the Asian Institute for Media Ministries (AIMM).

In 2013, a new GMC institute was launched, called the Institute for Church Action Against Poverty Studies (ICAPS), led by Filipino faculty member, Dr. Joel Tejedo, who had grown up begging for food in northern Luzon. For several years, he had been heading up a ministry of serving the poor in one of Baguio City's poorest areas, Lower Rock Quarry. He was also gaining recognition as an expert on ministries of social concern. This institute was designed to help workers in these ministries to think through different ways of serving the poor, as well as providing encouragement and fellowship among the workers.

Tham Wan Yee Becomes President

In 2009, APTS achieved a long-held dream in the appointment of its first non-AGWM president. Tham Wan Yee, along with his wife, Moon Tee Ngoh, were Malaysian AG missionaries, who had been serving at APTS since 2004. Their appointment followed a strong APTS tradition of promoting from within. Former presidents James Long, Dr. David Lim and Dr. John Carter had all been on the faculty when appointed as president, and even Dr. Cagle, though not a regular faculty member, had been involved in LDI on an annual basis as well as serving on the board. Before coming to APTS, Yee had served in Malaysia as a pastor and district superintendent and also had a background in business, giving him a wealth of experience that would enhance his role as president.

On July 29, 2009, APTS' 45th anniversary, he announced a five-year plan that would lead up to the 50th anniversary celebration in 2014 called the "Jubilee Vision." It also coincided with the centennial anniversary of the Assemblies of God, USA. His vision for APTS called for an enrollment goal of two hundred students, fourteen faculty with terminal degrees in their field, the development of a parcel of land on the south side of the campus into a prayer mountain, and the acquisition of a debt-free status, which included developing more revenue streams. The announcement and constant reiteration of this vision kept all administrators and faculty members flowing in the same direction. All of the goals would be achieved, but not necessarily by 2014.

Debt-free status was achieved when AGWM regional director for the Asia Pacific, Dr. J. Russell Turney, canceled the remaining debt owed to AGWM for the various construction projects, especially the ARC. In the Jubilee year of APTS, this news brought great jubilation to the APTS family!

Just the announcement of an intended prayer mountain brought an increased focus on prayer on campus. In 2012, a prayer mountain was developed on a rocky promontory just north of and below the new duplexes. Most of the area consisted of a large, grassy area, where people could walk and pray. Because of the stunning view of the valley, this also became a popular place to rent out for weddings. Dating and married couples also used it for courting in the evening. Five prayer "closets," along with a restroom, were constructed on the south side of the mountain so that those wishing could have a private place to pray.

In 2010, the Yees pioneered a GMC program for Chinese house church pastors, using their contacts among the five largest house church group networks in the People's Republic of China (PRC). This came at a strategic time when China was opening up in many ways. In the first year, about forty key house church leaders participated with the understanding that they would train others upon their return home and impact one of the largest unreached nations in the world. All classes were done in Mandarin. This became an annual event in which hundreds of pastors participated until the COVID-19 pandemic shut everything down in 2020. At first, sponsorship funds were raised to help defray the costs, but after three years, the Chinese themselves funded the program. The purpose for holding the program at APTS instead of somewhere in the PRC was to give Chinese leaders an opportunity to study without fear of harassment and to get them some exposure to the outside world, hopefully igniting with them a vision for other unreached nations.

Non-English Programs

For forty-eight years all classes at FEAST/APTS had been conducted in English. Now, with the stupendous need for trained workers in the People's Republic of China (PRC) and a multi-lingual Chinese-Malaysian president in place who had many connections to China's famous house church movement, plans for a program in Mandarin began to be laid. This was also consistent with APTS' long track record of being on the cutting edge of Pentecostal theological education in Asia and the fact that APTS' target market has occasionally shifted over the years.

Collaboration

Various memorandums of understanding were reached with various Bible schools and seminaries designed to provide for faculty or student exchanges and training for faculty members for various Bible schools. Some succeeded while others did not, but these MOUs signified APTS' strong commitment to collaboration and partnership with other institutions with similar goals and purposes.

The Jubilee Celebration

The Jubilee Celebration kicked off in February 2014, with a February edition of the *Asian Journal of Pentecostal Studies* dedicated to the theme "Jubilee Edition: Celebrating 50 Years of God's Faithfulness to the Asia Pacific Theological Seminary." Every contributor reflected on APTS's history, development, and impact since its inception in 1964.

The big event, however, was graduation, along with a special banquet, where many alumni returned to celebrate and reflect on what God had done. Dr. Prince Guneratnam, the former general superintendent of the AG in Malaysia and chairman of the World Pentecostal Fellowship, was the speaker for the occasion.

With a decade of service now under his belt, five of them as president, and with a full board, faculty, and staff in support, Tham Wan Yee now appointed to a second term was ready to lead into what God had for APTS in the future.

Zeal with Knowledge
The First Sixty Years of FEAST/APTS
Photo Gallery 3

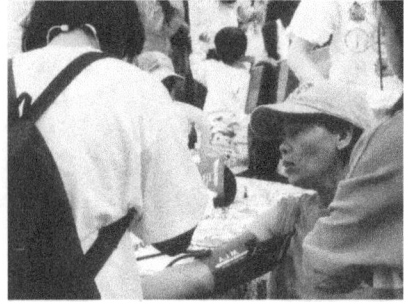
Medical Outreach Ministry in 2004

Koreans at International Night in 2004

Galen Preaching at APTS S. E. Week in 2004

Rev Tham Wan Yee Family in 2006

One of the two duplexes built in 2006

The other duplex

President Wayne Cagle Preaching in Chapel in 2006

Tham Wan Yee Graduates in 2006

Paul Lewis Hau Boy in 2006

Wonsuk Ma in 2006

Lectureship Banner in 2008

Spiritual Emphasis Week Worship in 2008

Central Luzon Extension Seminar in 2008

The Academic Research Center was dedicated in 2008

Aerial View of APTS in 2009

Judy Cagle, Amy Katelyn dela Cruz in 2009

Prayer Mountain Construction in 2011

Kay Fountain in 2009

Prayer Mountain The Prayer Closets are on the right but hidden from view

Dickie Hertweck Teaching English Writing in 2012

Chinese Group at the International Night in 2012

Chinese Graduates in 2016

Daniel Kelly's Wedding in 2014

Male Faculty Bonding Event at Starbucks in 2014 L to R Adrian Rosen, Richard Varnell, Dave Johnson, Galen Hertweck

President Tham Wan's Welcome Breakfast in 2014

Graduates in 2015

Korea Night at Coffee Bar in 2017

APTS Group Picture in 2018

Students in Chapel Service in 2018

Praying for the Nations at Hurst Chapel in 2018

Galen Hertweck Teaching in 2018

Gallery 3

NT Introduction Class in 2021

Online Faculty Prayer Meeting in 2021

Online students are required to have a second camera for exams

Cross on Prayer Mountain in 2023

Kids on Campus in 2023

Selah Night in October 2023

Kitchen's Maintenance Crew in January 2023

Incroming President Solomon Wang and his wife, Lori, represent the future of APTS

International, Pentecostal, and Missional: (2014-2024)

At the annual board meeting in 2014, the president, Dr. Tham Wan Yee, was appointed to a new five-year term and would be appointed to a third term in 2019. By the end of 2014, there were twenty-four resident faculty members. While only ten had doctorates, another six were working on their terminal degrees. Prayer Mountain was also in operation and the school was debt-free, meaning that two of Dr. Yee's goals had been attained.

For Dr. Tham Wan Yee, the Pentecostal distinctives of APTS could be seen in the campus layout and calendar events. Prayer Mountain illustrates a commitment to spiritual formation, the ARC to the realm of academics, and the GMC to practical ministry outreaches. This was mirrored by calendar events such as Spiritual Emphasis Week (spiritual formation), the annual Menzies Lectureship (academics), and the annual Missions Convention (outreach and practical ministry), in addition to the routine events of chapel, classes, and ministry opportunities. The academic dean, Dr. Kay Fountain, echoed this in her belief that academic excellence, ministry, and character formation can and should be integrated into the lives of faculty and students. All of this represents APTS' commitment to a balanced Pentecostal spirituality of sound doctrine, practical ministry, and passionate spirituality.

The president also continued his efforts to identify new markets for APTS. In 2014, he launched the Mekong Initiative as a replacement for the China Initiatives to attract students from the countries through which the famed river flows, namely Myanmar, Thailand, Cambodia, Laos, and Vietnam, by offering them a specific scholarship. The total population of this region is around 240 million people with many Unreached People Groups. Buddhism is the dominant religion. At the time of this writing, ten students had taken advantage of this opportunity: three from Myanmar, four from Vietnam, and one each from Thailand, Laos and Cambodia.

The president also continued his participation in various interfaith dialogues. A Lutheran-Pentecostal dialogue was held on campus in 2016, and, in 2019, APTS hosted the Pentecostal-Reformed dialogue. While the dialogues themselves were closed to the faculty and students, one chapel session was dedicated to a panel discussion in which the members of the dialogue answered questions from APTS chapel participants.

The student body number had not yet reached the goal of two-hundred, but it also represented a wide range of backgrounds. In the 2018-2019 school year, the registrar's office reported that sixty-two denominations and church traditions were represented in the student body, although the majority were from various AG bodies across Asia and the Pacific.

Alphacrucis College (AC)

Part of Dr. Tham Wan Yee's strategy for resourcing APTS was to form a partnership with Alphacrucis College (now Alphacrucis University College), in Sydney, Australia. Alphacrucis College (AC) was already in expansion mode by adding several branch locations throughout Australia and elsewhere. APTS already had a good relationship with AC, mainly through APTA, but also because the president of AC is a member of the APTS board of directors. Not only could a branch of AC potentially bring students into APTS, but the APTS share of the financial resources involved could also be used to support the seminary. Moreover, the program would offer majors in business and missions and a bachelor's in ministry, meaning that it was consistent with APTS' purpose and values. Since AC itself is the national school of the Australian Christian Churches (Assemblies of God), there was no problem with doctrinal issues or other values. One advantage for the students was getting a fully accredited degree from a Western institution while living in Asia. The program was launched in January, 2020, with seven students.

Postgraduate Programs

In 2019, a new D.Min. extension began in Singapore. Overall, the D.Min. has been the largest of the postgraduate programs in terms of students and graduates. The M.Th. underwent renovation at about the same time with the hope of better addressing the students' expressed desire to spend at least a portion of their program in class with other students.

In March 2014, the board approved a new Ph.D. program that the postgraduate program had been deliberating over for some time. This would be the first time since the closure of the APTS-UWB split program in 2009 that APTS had a Ph.D. program and it was the first time they had set out to do this alone. Again, this was part of APTS' long-standing commitment to be on the cutting edge of AG theological education in the Asia Pacific. Like any program, many issues had to be worked through and resolved but the program has borne solid fruit so far and shows great potential for the future.

The structure of the program made it ideal for those in full-time ministry who wished to pursue serious and sustained academic research. Except for two research courses, which could be done by independent study, the entire program could be done while engaged in ministry. While they were required to come to campus for six to eight weeks a year, they could apply for an exemption if they could demonstrate that they had sufficient library resources and time for study where they were. In 2019, Darin Clements, an AGWM missionary to Cambodia, became the first graduate of the program. More have followed since then. Over the last decade, a small but steady stream of students have finished their postgraduate degrees and returned home to invest their lives in others.

Chinese Degree Program

In June, 2014, APTS opened a new degree, a 120-hour B.A., and a 36-hour M.A. degree program in the Mandarin language to help meet the staggering need for well-educated Christian leaders in China. The program was led by Dr. Joe Liu, a missionary from the AG in Taiwan and his wife, Lana. This was the first degree program in the history of APTS that was done in a language other than English. Eleven students from China and Taiwan originally enrolled and the first group graduated in 2016. By this time, the program was already accredited with ATESEA.

Faculty

The faculty, many of them having administrative responsibilities as well as teaching classes, continued to bear the bulk of the work at APTS. Some positions, such as the business administrator and registrar, were considered non-teaching faculty. The professional competence of the faculty was well established not only by their academic qualifications but also by upgrading their knowledge in the relevant fields and delivery technologies. Their continuing efforts in publication, coupled with the seminary's journal and book publishing, have made the seminary a center for Pentecostal studies in Asia. Faculty members are viewed by the students as their role models in life and ministry. The resident campus life provides an environment conducive for mentoring relationships and the student-to-teacher ratio was an excellent five to one, meaning that the faculty had the opportunity to develop significant relationships with the students.

In addition to their regular duties, a number of faculty were involved in either the AGST consortium or APTA, or taught block courses in Bible schools as well as the APTS extensions, expanding the impact of APTS well beyond the Baguio City campus.

Faculty Transitions (2014-2023)

Continuing Service

Dr. Tom and Connie Bohnert continued to serve at APTS, although they eventually moved to Manila due to the educational needs of their children, and Tom returned to teach block courses. He also served as the extension director, now known as the director for distance learning, until 2021. Dr. Galen and Dickie Hertweck continued their service during this period. In 2021, Dr. Hertweck reassumed the role of director for distance learning, and, in 2023, Dickie became head of the ELP in which she had already taught for many years.

Dr. Tham Wan Yee and Moon Tee Ngoh also served during the entire period and announced their intention to step down as president at the 60th Anniversary celebration in 2024, which coincides with the conclusion of his third term as president. Jun and Jane Kim also continued their ministry at APTS. Jun served as the dean of students from 2015-16 and later became the associate academic dean. He became the interim academic dean in 2020 when Dr. Teresa Chai passed away and was fully appointed to the position a year later. Joel and Carolyn Tejedo continued their service, with Carolyn handling the registrar's role from 2014-19 and Joel took on the responsibilities of the APRC in 2019 and the library in 2023. Dr. Joe and Lana Liu continued to lead the Chinese program, although they had to return to Taiwan due to visa issues. They have continued to serve both online and on campus for almost half of each year during key times for the Chinese department. Dr. Dave and Debbie Johnson have also served the whole time. Debbie became the dean of students in 2017 and continued to direct the ELP until 2020, when the two jobs became too much for her. In November, 2023, she resigned from the dean of students role but continues to be a teacher in the ELP. Dr. Weldyn Houger has continued to teach online from the United States and served as the director of the postgraduate programs until 2023. Dr. Barb Houger continued to teach and oversee the D.Min. program until she retired from the faculty in 2021. Marlene Yap also continued to teach Greek.

Departures

Herman Dionson resigned in 2015 to pursue other ministry opportunities. The head librarian, Nick Wilson, went to be with the Lord in 2016 and his wife, Ruth, did not continue with AGWM. Also in 2017, Drs. Richard and Joy Varnell had to step down because of his health issues, although she continued to edit for the Press until 2022. In 2018, Dr. Kay Fountain, the academic dean, retired to New Zealand after twenty-three years of faithful service, making her second only to Dr. Wonsuk Ma in tenure on the faculty. Im Seok (David) Kang and his wife, Jin Young Ngo, also resigned in 2020 to become missionaries to Indonesia. Dr. Teresa Chai succeeded Dr. Fountain as the academic dean in 2018 and served faithfully until her death from cancer in March, 2020. Hirokatsu and Miyuki Yoshihara returned permanently to Japan in 2021.

Arrivals

Dr. Adrian and Stephanie Rosen came in 2014 and Adrian taught New Testament courses while completing his Ph.D. at AGTS in Springfield, Missouri. He also served as the M.Th. coordinator from 2019-22, after which they returned to the USA to teach in a Bible school there. Lindsay Crabtree came in 2014 and taught in the English program and later came under the faculty-in-training program. She met and married a student, Moon Hyun Choi. They departed in 2016 to the USA to pursue full missionary appointment. Jason Williams and his wife, Jane, who had served in China, joined the faculty from 2014-17. Jason taught missions and Jane research methods, but they could not continue because of Jason's serious health issues.

Daniel Qin taught briefly from 2014-2015, while completing his M.Th. at APTS and married fellow student Kelly Huang. They departed in 2015 to pursue further studies in Edinburgh, UK. Stephen Yao and his wife, Enhui Li (Grace), continued at APTS after graduating in 2016. He taught in the Chinese program until 2022 when they moved to Israel for him to pursue postgraduate studies. Dr. Youjin Chung and his wife, Bea Kyunghwa, arrived from Korea in 2017 and he taught Systematic Theology and Church History. He also served a short stint as library coordinator in 2019. Affiliated with a Baptist organization in Korea, he was the first appointed regular faculty member in the history of APTS who was personally Pentecostal, but not AG. They departed in 2019, but he continued as an adjunct.

Dr. Bob and Marilyn Stefan (AGWM) came to APTS as MAs (missionary associates) from 1998-2001. Bob served on the faculty, raised funds for APTS, and taught church management and fundraising for ministry. They returned to APTS from 2017 to 2019 and were considered regular faculty although, as self-funded missionaries, they needed to spend much of the year in the USA tending to business interests. Dr. Stefan taught subjects like a biblical perspective on wealth and possessions, among other things, and Marilyn was instrumental in pursuing the partnership with Alphacrucis College, CHED recognition, and directed the online courses. However, they had to step down in 2020 due to unfortunate personal circumstances beyond their control. Ed and Dr. Sherry Benish also arrived in 2017. He is the current business administrator and Sherry taught in the ELP, serving as its director from 2020-23 and currently is pioneering a new ministry on campus, the International Language Center, which offers classes in a variety of languages.

Byeoung-kuk Kim and his wife, Eunsil Tae, came in 2016 and Byeoung-kuk enrolled in the Faculty in Training program. They left during the COVID-19 pandemic due to a family crisis and were not able to continue. Lora Timenia, a Filipina, joined the faculty under the Faculty Development Program in 2017 while she was engaged in the M.Th. program at APTS. In time, she married Karlo Timenia, one of the students. She taught research methods and Pentecostal/Charismatic studies. From 2019-21 she also served as the registrar before moving to the USA to pursue a Ph.D. at Oral Roberts University. Alumna Grace Wu Kumi started teaching research methods, essay writing, and intercultural studies in the Chinese program in 2017 and later married fellow student, Francis Kumi, from Ghana.

Dr. Li-Hua (Laura Sun), from Taiwan, joined the faculty in 2018 and taught missions subjects, first in the Chinese program and more recently, the English. Jibin Liu (Nehemiah) and Xinhua Yu (Grace), his wife, came from China in 2019 to teach ministry and counseling courses in the Chinese program. Drs. Stuart and Kathleen Rochester, natives of Australia, joined the faculty in 2020. Stuart teaches New Testament and Hermeneutics courses and Kathleen teaches Old Testament and Counseling. He also serves as the coordinator for the M.Th. and Ph.D. programs. APTS graduate Elavaya Oseso joined the Faculty Development Program in 2020 and taught Hebrew and research methods. She was also the interim dean of students for one school year. She and her husband, Tony, are from Kenya and he is the chaplain for the Alphacrucis program. Dr. Darin and Dianna Clements, veteran AGWM missionaries to Cambodia, joined APTS in 2020. They both taught in the intercultural education program. Dianna joined the faculty when she finished her D.Min. in 2022. She also became the director of the GMC programs. Darin initially also served as the coordinator for the D.Min. and Ph.D. programs, but later stepped down from the Ph.D. program. Dr. William Toh and his wife, Tina Oh, came from Singapore in 2022. William taught ministry and leadership.

Dr. David Han, accompanied by his wife, Lydia Park, joined the faculty in 2021 and taught missions courses. Born in Korea, they spent many years working with indigenous peoples in Canada prior to coming to APTS. Claudia Mendoza Rodriguez became the first Latino to teach (missions courses) at APTS in 2021 as part of the Faculty Development Program while pursuing her Ph.D. at APTS. Grace Shen Elizaga, from China, accompanied by her husband, Ryan, a Filipino, began teaching ministry courses in the Chinese program in 2021. Jemon Subang, accompanied by his wife, Myra, from the Philippines, joined the Faculty Development Program in 2021 and teaches Greek. Yijun (Amos) Chen, accompanied by his wife, Meng Dong (Deborah), enrolled in the Faculty-in-Training Program in 2022 and taught Church History and ministry courses in the Chinese program. Shannell Hsueh (AGWM) came from Taiwan to teach in the Chinese program and the ELP while her husband, David, studied. She also completed a degree. Li Zhang started teaching ministry courses in the Chinese Program in 2023, accompanied by his wife, Rachel Luo.

As usual, a small army of non-resident regular and adjunct faculty members continued to fill gaps and teach in areas where APTS did not have qualified faculty or needed additional faculty to cover the workload. While space does not permit mentioning all of their names, collectively they made a sizable contribution to the success of APTS. Two of these, however, deserve special mention due to their length of service. Everett and Evelyn McKinney, who served as APTS president and faculty member, respectively, from 1977-1984, have continued to serve in other ways, mostly as regular non-resident faculty members, ever since, meaning that their association with APTS has now spanned forty-seven years! The names of the others who served in these capacities from 2004-23 can be found in Appendices C and D.

Registration

Enrollment continued to be steady throughout the decade, although Dr. Yee's goal of reaching 200 students enrolled at the main campus was not achieved until the COVID-19 pandemic hit and all classes went online.

TABLE 5.

RESIDENT CAMPUS		EXTENSION		TOTAL ENROLLMENT
ACADEMIC YEAR	ENROLLMENT	CALENDAR YEAR	ENROLLMENT	
2014-2015	138	2014	38	176
2015-2016	183	2015	55	238
2016-2017	180	2016	54	234
2017-2018	152	2017	38	190
2018-2019	157	2018	63	220
2019-2020	162	2019	56	218
2020-2021	195	2020	13	208
2021-2022	242	2021	17	259
2022-2023	255	2022	8	263
2023-2024 (1st-2nd Trimester only)	212	2023 (June-December 2023 only)	14	226

Outstanding Students

Every year, the faculty recognizes two outstanding students, one at the M.A. level, the other at the M.Div. The awardees from 2014-23 at the M.A. level were Elizabeth Ashley Pell (USA), Zhang Li (China), Dorothy Elavaya Oseso (Kenya), Sushil Sharma (Nepal), Aires Mia Amor Rodriguez (Philippines), Yee Meng Chew (Malaysia), Ane Sesimoni Soraya Aipolo (Tonga), and Archie Arapan Manoto (Philippines). The M.Div level awardees were Stephen Sein Shwe (Myanmar), Sunil Singh (Nepal), Huang Qun Huan (China), Epineri Vulakouvaki (Fiji Islands), Sukjin Lee (Korea), Madhuri Rana (Nepal), Qiu Wenyu (China), Daniel Abel Morisa (USA), and Joan Faith Calumpang (Philippines). Jemon Subang (Philippines) and Sarah Joy Caballero (Philippines) won the award at both levels when they completed these respective degrees.

Library

Our Filipino staff has continued to provide excellent library service. One of the priorities of the library during this time has been the acquisition of doctoral dissertations, whether in digital or printed format. The sheer number of dissertations done by Asians that are currently available supports the fact that APTS is an excellent place to study Asian Pentecostalism. The library and the *Asian Journal of Pentecostal Studies* partnered with as many as sixty-five other journals in a journal exchange program that added journals to the library at a low cost.

The library also maintained professional memberships with the Baguio Benguet Theological Library Association and the Philippine Theological Library Association, both of which provided an inter-library loan service for its members. As APTS began to consider offering programs in other languages, books in those languages became a strong need. In response to this, $20,000 was donated from Taiwan and $10,000 from the AGWM Northern Asia office to start a Chinese library. A Korean pastor donated 1,500 books to begin a

Korean library. These libraries now occupy the space that used to hold the old library. As of November, 2023, the library held the following:

TABLE 6.

Number of Books (English collection)	62,693 vols.
Dissertations/Theses	1,044 vols.
CD/DVD's	133 vols.
Vertical files Items	1,954 titles
Periodicals (bound Journal, Magazines and Newspapers)	
Total no. of volumes	22,360 vols.
Total no. of Titles (*not including EBSCO)	2,337 titles
Chinese collections	4,247 vols.
Magazines (in Mandarin)	192 titles
Korean collections	2,760 vols.

The Asia Pacific Research Center (APRC)

The main work of the APRC during this time was a project in which Dr. Joel Tejedo, the director of the APRC, participated. Dr. Tejedo, a member of a global research team funded by the John Templeton Foundation in the USA, was studying megachurches worldwide. As the leader of the Filipino team, he studied and conducted extensive field research on megachurches in the Metro Manila region. He also traveled widely to present the research findings and published some of them in the *Asian Journal of Pentecostal Studies*.

Faculty Development Program

Between 2014 and 2023, five faculty members completed their postgraduate degrees. In 2017, Joe Liu completed his Ph.D. in developmental education from the University of Baguio and Im Seok (David) Kang received his M.Th. in Old Testament from the AGST in 2020. Also in 2020, Lora Timenia finished her M.Th. from APTS in Pentecostal/Charismatic studies, and her thesis was subsequently published through APTS Press. In 2021, Jun Kim completed his Ph.D.

in historical theology from the Oxford Center for Missions Studies in the UK and Marlene Yap finished her M.Th. in biblical studies from the AGST. Others entered the program during this time. The variety of fields of study represented here will strengthen the school for years to come.

Extension Program (Tom Bohnert)

Also during this period, an extension was opened in a restricted access nation. In 2017, the board of directors approved a new extension in Thailand to be conducted in the Thai language. This was the first and, to date, only extension offered in a language other than English, although some classes in the Myanmar extension were also taught in Burmese. The first students graduated during the 2019-20 school year. As of 2021, other extensions were being held in American Samoa, Fiji, Mongolia, New Zealand, Western Samoa, and California, although COVID-19 restrictions at the time put all of them on hold and the extension students were encouraged to join the online classes broadcasted from Baguio City.

APTS Press and the *Asian Journal of Pentecostal Studies*

When Dr. Dave Johnson first became the managing editor of the Journal and director of the Press in 2012, he and Debbie were living in southern Luzon and became non-resident, regular faculty members. When they moved to Baguio City in April 2013 to become resident faculty members, Dr. Tham Wan Yee, the president, and Dr. Kay Fountain, the academic dean, committed to allowing Dave up to 75 percent of his time to do publishing, demonstrating the school's commitment to this ministry. Under his leadership, the two books mentioned in the previous chapter were published in 2013.

In 2014, *Understanding the Iglesia ni Cristo: What They Really Believe and How They Can Be Reached*, by Dr. Anne Harper from the AGST, was published as part of the newly inaugurated APTS Monographs Series which also included books by Drs. Johnson and Turney. This reflected APTS' desire to publish theses and dissertations, targeting pastors, Bible school instructors, and other church leaders in Asia. The second book published that year was *Pentecostal Pioneer: The Life and Legacy of Rudy Esperanza* and *The Early Years of the Assemblies of God in the Philippines*, by Dr. Dynnice Rosanny Engcoy. This was published as part of the Pentecost Around the World Series. The third book published in 2014, *A Theology of the Spirit in Doctrine and Demonstration: Essays in Honor of Wonsuk and Julie Ma*, edited by APTS faculty member, Dr. Teresa Chai, was the first festschrift ever published by APTS.

In 2016, the Press published another festschrift entitled: *Theological Education in a Cross-Cultural Context: Essays in Honor of John and Bea Carter*, edited by Dr. Fountain, to mark the occasion of their 25th and final year of their affiliation with APTS. Also in 2016, a reprint of the 2004 book, *David Yonggi Cho: A Close Look at His Theology & Ministry*, was also released. *Pentecostals and the Poor: Reflections From the Indian Context*, by Dr. Ivan Satyavrata, was published in 2017. This was also the first of a new series commissioned by the Press called the Occasional Papers Series, where journal-length articles could be published as small books either by one author or several. In 2018, the Press published its third festschrift, *The Old Testament in Theology and Teaching: Essays in Honor of Kay Fountain*, edited by Drs. Teresa Chai and Dave Johnson, which was presented to her upon her retirement at graduation. *A Theology of Hope: Contextual Perspectives in Korean Pentecostalism*, by Dr. Sang Yun Lee, became the fourth book in the APTS Press Monograph Series. The Press also released a new expanded edition of Dr. Roger Stronstad's book, *Spirit, Scripture and Theology: A Pentecostal Perspective*, which had been the first book published by the Press in 1995. This edition was later translated into Mandarin and Spanish through arrangements with Mandarin and Spanish language publishers.

In March 2019, the fourth festschrift was published entitled, *Training Asians to Reach the World: Essays Honoring Everett and Evelyn McKinney for 50 Years in Missions*, edited by Dr. Dave Johnson. Joshua Lovelace's book, *Seedtime to Harvest: The History of the Assemblies of God in Cambodia*, became the fifth book in the Pentecost Around the World Series in 2019. Faculty member Dr. Robert Stefan's book, *Business in Islam: Contextualizing Business and Mission in Muslim-*

Majority Nations, became the fifth volume of the Monograph Series and was also published in 2019.

In 2020, the Press produced a stand-alone book by Dr. Arto Hämäläinen and Ulf Strohben entitled, *To the Ends of the Earth: Building a National Missionary Sending Structure*. Two more volumes of the APTS Press Monograph Series were also published that year: *A Multimedia Literacy Project Toward Biblical Literacy in Bangladesh*, by Dr. Teresa Chai (posthumously) and *Third Wave Pentecostalism in the Philippines: Understanding Toronto Blessing Revivalism's Signs and Wonders Theology in the Philippines*, by Lora Timenia. Dr. Craig Keener's book, *For All Peoples: A Biblical Theology of Missions in the Gospels and Acts*, a publication of the lectures that he had given in 2009 at the annual APTS Menzies Lectureship, became the second book in the Occasional Papers Series.

In 2021, Dr. Youjin Chung's book, *Reformation From Below: Looking at Münster Anabaptism Anew Through Korean Minjung Theology*, became the eighth book in the Monograph Series. In 2022, the Press released the first of what is hoped to be a three-volume, multi-author work entitled, *Pentecostal Theological Education in the Majority World: The Graduate and Post-Graduate Level*. Volume two will be on the baccalaureate level and the third volume, if produced, will be on non-formal theological education. Also in 2022, Dr. Robert Banks' book, The *Versatility of Paul: Artisan Missioner, Community Developer, Pastoral Educator*, which he originally gave as lectures at the 2021 Menzies Lectureship, was published as the third book in the Occasional Papers Series. In 2023, the Press released a reprint of Dr. Tavita Pagaialii's 2006 book, the third in the Pentecost Around the World Series, *Pentecost Unto the Uttermost: A History of the Assemblies of God in Samoa*. By the end of 2023, fifty-two editions of the *Asian Journal of Pentecostal Studies* had been published, all giving evidence to APTS' strong commitment to publishing on the theological, missiological, historical, and practical ministry issues current in Asia.

In 2013 the Press began expanding its readership by selling books on Amazon Kindle and later added paperback editions, giving global exposure to APTS. In 2014, an agreement was signed with Wipf and Stock Publishers, a well-respected academic publisher in the USA, to co-publish APTS Press books, giving APTS Press greater access to the

North American market and the ability to use their brand in marketing Press books. In 2018, the Press hired its first full-time marketing assistant. The results were encouraging. From 2013-2023, the only years for which sales records were available, over 18,000 books were sold. Also in 2018, on a separate website for the Press and Journal, www.aptspress.org, APTS Press books were advertised with clickable links to Amazon, and the Journal could be downloaded without cost. Later, Journal accounts were added on academia.edu, ResearchGate, and AMRIConnect.net, which resulted in significantly wider exposure of the Press and Journal. When shipping was interrupted due to COVID-19 and the price of postage skyrocketed when it became available again, the decision was made to discontinue the print edition and publish only online, reflecting a change already in place for many similar journals.

In 2017, the Press launched a vision to give books to Bible schools all over Asia, regardless of Christian tradition or denominational affiliation. By the end of 2023, the Press had distributed 2,552 books to over two-hundred Bible schools and seminaries in over thirty nations, all but a few of them in Asia.

Commission on Higher Education (CHED) and (TESDA)

After a lot of work, the Philippine Commission on Higher Education (CHED) recognized five programs in 2018 for the first time: the D.Min., M.Th., M.A. in Ministry, M.Div. and M.A. in Intercultural Studies with Islamic concentration. This has proven to be a great asset in getting both student and missionary visas. The APTS extension program, however, was not included. In 2023, the ELP was accredited by the Technical Education and Skills Development (TESDA), the Philippine government agency that oversees non-academic programs, which also helped those in the program to gain student visas.

William W. Menzies Annual Lectureship

The Annual Menzies Lectureship continued to provide faculty and students with the opportunity to hear top scholars in their fields and probe deep theological and missiological current issues. While there were many occasions for exploring Pentecostal distinctives, a number of scholars from outside the Pentecostal movement were also invited, giving all a wider view of the kingdom of God. Lecturers included Drs. Al Tizon, 2015; Donald Hagner, 2016; Waldemar Kowalski, 2017; Cecil M. Robeck Jr., 2018; Cheryl Bridges Johns, 2019; Ben Witherington III, 2020; Robert Banks, 2021; Melba P. Maggay, 2022; Wonsuk and Julie Ma, 2023 and, at the time of this writing, Dr. Frank Macchia is planning to come in 2024. In 2021 and 2022, the lectureship was only online due to the COVID-19 pandemic and, in 2023, it was done in a hybrid format, with on-campus personnel attending in person and others attending online.

Other Missionaries on Campus

Departures

Sunil Kuan and his wife retired in the USA in 2015. In 2017, Kent and Paige Parrish left to become missionaries to Indonesia. Fa Chi (Andrew) Mo and his wife, Alice Huang, concluded their time at APTS in 2018 and returned to Taiwan.

Arrivals

Jocelyn Green (AGWM) taught one trimester in the ELP in 2016 and then from 2022-23 before returning to the USA to get married. Molly Peng came from Taiwan from 2016-2020 to assist in the Chinese program. Along the way she married Guang Ming Li, a student from China, and went on to pursue other ministries in China and Taiwan after he graduated. Karen Malsack taught English in 2016 but unfortunately passed away that same year. Daniel and Kazune Matsunaga (AGWM) served briefly from 2017-18. Daniel taught in the ELP and served as the assistant dean of students before they returned to Japan to continue their ministry there. Eunice Angeles (AGWM) taught in the ELP from 2019-22 before returning to the USA to pursue full missions appointment. David Lee, accompanied by his wife, Beau, taught in the ELP from 2019-2021 and then returned to Korea. Sha Yu (Mandy) and her husband, Jason Zhou, came from China in 2019 and Mandy serves in both the Alphacrucis Program and the Chinese Program. In 2023, Diego Alvarez and his wife, Deissy Palacio, veteran missionaries from Argentina, joined the APTS team to serve in the new ILC program and to liaise with AG in councils in Latin America who want to send their missionaries who will serve in Asia to study in the English program or one of the degree programs.

Campus Life

The student coffee bar, manned by volunteers from the student body under the leadership of the student council, was open several hours a week. Students are often seen talking, studying, using the Internet, and even playing games there. The children on campus often came for their own individual or group activities or to study.

One of the social highlights of the year is the all-school outing, which was normally held during the third trimester at a resort outside of Baguio City in places where multiple sports, including swimming, could be played. This afforded an excellent opportunity for the faculty and student body to relax together outside of the pressures of academics. Since the end of the COVID-19 pandemic, this event has morphed into occasional sports fests right on campus.

The school also offered a medical clinic when medical professionals were available. Several of the nurses came from qualified students or spouses and local doctors occasionally donated their services. A nursery for small campus and staff children was provided for a time, with parents shouldering the expenses.

One of the many benefits of chapel services three times a week was that there was ample opportunity for students to participate and gain experience in leading worship services. Also, many graduating students had the opportunity to preach before they graduated, allowing the faculty to see the fruit of their labors. Communion was served at the beginning and end of most trimesters. Special nights for prayer or worship were also occasionally organized by the student council.

Small groups on Fridays, in lieu of chapel, provided another place where students and faculty could spend downtime together, normally in the home of a faculty member. Those leading and hosting the small groups were given the liberty to do what they wanted during that time. Some played games, others just visited and some had valuable discussions on various issues and sometimes the meetings were focused on prayer. The ability to do this right on campus set APTS apart from most other seminaries, where the faculty and, often, the students live off campus.

Several prayer groups formed on their own, whether it was the students from the various nations gathering or Jummah prayer for Muslims on Friday. Prayer Mountain has also been well used for those who want to spend time seeking the Lord.

The GMC

All of the summer GMC institutes continued without interruption except the Missionary Training Program, which was discontinued for a time and restarted in 2017 until 2019 as the Missionary Training Institute. In 2016, a new institute was started, originally under the name Children's Ministries Institute (CMI), now known as Ministry to Children Asia Pacific (MCAP). Many of these institutes were done in partnership with organizations that specialized in each ministry.

In 2023, the International Language Center (ILC) program was launched under the direction of Dr. Sherry Benish. The ILC aims to linguistically (and culturally) empower missionaries and their families to spread the good news even more effectively. Because APTS is an international community, ILC students and their families also have excellent exposure to a multicultural environment on campus. The schedule is flexible and can be adapted to the needs of the students. The major difference between the English program of the ILC and the ELP is that the ELP focuses on preparing students to study using theological English for seminary classes whereas the ILC does not. Another goal of the ILC was to generate internal revenue for APTS. Two pilot courses were offered in the January-March term, but there were only two students who wanted to study Tagalog. The summer term included nine students, all studying English.

TABLE 7.

	INSTITUTE	TOTALS
1	Asia Pacific Institute of Buddhist Studies	55
2	Asian Institute of Media Ministries	54
3	Asian Institute of Youth Studies	271
4	Christian Counseling Program	52
5	English Language Institute	35
6	Leadership Development Institute	91
7	Ministry to Children Asia Pacific (formerly Children's Ministry Institute)	273
8	Missionary Training Program	312
9	Special English Course	8
10	Institute for Islamic Studies (from 1998)	1,240

Business Office and Staff Operations

The APTS business office and staff members continued their efforts to keep all operations running smoothly, making sure everything on campus was well maintained, including faculty and student housing. Our staff hosted groups using the GMC, maintained the grounds, cared for the vehicles of those who had them, provided food service, and served faculty, visitors, and students in various offices and the bookstore. They also performed repairs on everything from buildings to toasters, accomplished renovation work and a myriad of other tasks not always seen by casual observers. House G, which was quite large, was divided into a faculty duplex during this time.

While APTS does most of its own maintenance, it keeps a list of contractors in the area that can be called in for specific jobs. The school is highly respected in the community as one that honors its contracts and pays its bills on time. A list of the staff members who have served a minimum of ten years can be found in Appendix B at the back of the book. The business administrators worked hard to ensure that the staff was adequately compensated to the best of the school's ability, including appropriate medical and retirement benefits. Their contribution to the mission of APTS, although not always recognized, has been significant.

Maintaining safety and security is also a high priority. In this case, APTS has found it beneficial to contract with outside security firms to provide guards for the campus and monitor the CCTV cameras placed in strategic places. On at least one occasion, the staff participated in a basic firefighting orientation and basic cardiopulmonary resuscitation (CPR) training conducted by the Baguio City Fire Department.

The campus also maintains its own, regularly tested, well water system, although many on campus prefer to purchase mineral water or put filters on their faucets. Generator backup systems are maintained for whenever there is a power outage in the area. The school has also made a continued effort to upgrade internet technology on campus, including the installation of outdoor routers. The online Moodle educational platform is used for classes.

COVID-19

Like everybody else, APTS was not prepared for COVID-19. In March, 2020, the Philippine government ordered a complete shutdown of all schools, even though APTS was only weeks from graduation, which resulted in its cancellation. Classes and final exams suddenly had to be conducted online via Zoom. While APTS was already doing six classes online, most of the faculty had no experience in this medium of education. All summer institutes were cancelled, as there simply was not enough time to figure out how to do them well online. Some were done online in 2021 but were not resumed in person until 2023.

Baguio City and the surrounding communities went into lockdown and travel off campus was restricted to certain hours on assigned days and the only places open were grocery stores, pharmacies, and hospitals, to deal with the essentials of life. Carpooling for grocery shopping became a necessity. A couple of co-ops were also organized with businesses that could deliver groceries to the campus. Social distancing and contact tracing policies were strictly enforced in the outside community. Travel outside the city was restricted to family emergencies and permits had to be approved by the mayor's office. Various police checkpoints were established, one just outside the campus gate, to ensure compliance with all ordinances and policies.

Initially, all air, bus, and boat travel to other islands was shut down, leaving many stranded, including a Filipino graduate who could not get home. By the time the new school year opened in June, 2021, international air travel had somewhat reopened to allow tourists and foreign students to go home, although none were allowed into the country. Since classes could only be done online, dozens of students took the opportunity to go home and study from there. The campus population dropped so low that the cafeteria had to be closed, forcing dorm students to move into the then-vacant apartments. The maintenance department took advantage of this situation to do extensive renovations in apartments and dorms in Bethesda.

Because being at home led to more family and church responsibilities, some of the full-time students switched to part-time. However, now that all programs were online, enrollment increased significantly. Free tuition during this time was also a major factor. Graduation was held online in 2021-22 and included 2020 graduates as well since graduation had to be cancelled. Chapel services were reduced from three times a week to once a week due to technical issues online.

For the most part, everyone on campus responded calmly to the situation and relied heavily on God's grace and one another to get through the crisis. When someone had to be quarantined because of contracting COVID-19 or having been exposed to it, others pitched in to deliver groceries, medicines, or whatever else needed to be done.

The local economy, much of it based on tourism, was hit hard due to the lockdown. Unemployment rose to 40 percent in Baguio City and was as high as 90 percent near campus, since most of the local people in the area of the school were employed in the tourist trade. By God's grace and provision, none of the staff at APTS had to be laid off, although some did have to work in other departments on campus. On two occasions, the faculty and students raised funds internally to provide food for the needy in the local community.

The country began to slowly reopen in early 2022 under the watchful eye of the Department of Health and the campus slowly came back to its normal, vibrant life. The cafeteria was reopened part-time at first and resumed full service as more students returned or arrived to begin studies. In-person classes resumed in September 2022, and the faculty decided that the online courses would continue, converting them into a hybrid format. In 2023, in-person graduation resumed and those who graduated in the three previous years were invited to come back and walk the line if they desired and some of them did so. Most of the summer institutes resumed in-person classes as well. As the country continued to re-open, organizations booked the GMC for their meetings again and weddings on campus resumed.

Conclusion

As APTS prepares to celebrate its 60th anniversary in March 2024, where this revised edition will be launched, there is much for which to be thankful. The number of alumni as of 2023 now stands at 1,434, with more expected to graduate during the anniversary ceremonies. Many have gone on to hold significant leadership positions in the AG throughout the Asia Pacific and Pacific Oceania regions and, no doubt, all have made an impact for Christ in one way or another in various ministry assignments that they have held over the years. Only eternity will reveal the total impact of their lives. Over the last sixty years, missionaries from all across Asia and the West have given countless years of their lives for Christ's cause at APTS, supported by friends, families, and churches in their homelands. Countless Filipino staff have served God at APTS. At the graduation in 2024, when Tham Wan Yee and Moon Tee Ngoh step down as president and first lady of APTS after twenty years of service, fifteen of them as president, Dr. Solomon Wang and his wife, Lori, missionaries with AGWM, will pick up the reins and lead APTS into the future.

As this book goes to press, the task of world evangelization remains unfinished. Three billion people in over 7,400 people groups have never heard the gospel and have little access to it. Many of them are in Asia. This task remains urgent. The work of APTS must go on until Jesus comes again.

Zeal with Knowledge
The First Sixty Years of FEAST/APTS

Appendices

APPENDIX A
APTS ALUMNI RECORD (1966 - 2023)

LAST NAME	FIRST NAME	HOME COUNTRY	DEGREE	YEAR GRANTED
Marcos	Jaime Casticimo	Philippines	B. Th.	1966
Reyes	Tommy Yaneza	Philippines	B. Th.	1966
Bercero	Eduardo Z.	Philippines	B. Th.	1967
Cruz	Virginia C.	Philippines	B. Th.	1967
Nair	Gigeon Gopalan	Fiji	B. Th.	1967
Resus	Mateo D.	Philippines	B. Th.	1967
Sulpico	Valentia Urriza	Philippines	B. Th.	1967
Fernandez	Cresmerio B.	Philippines	B. Th.	1968
Ganalongo	Marina P.	Philippines	B. Th. M.A.	1968 1991
Indangan	Demetrio E.	Philippines	B.R.E. B. Th.	1968 1969
Karunapala	Marshall Nitawala	Sri Lanka	B. Th.	1968
Lontoh	San Goan (Samuel)	Indonesia	B. Th. M.A. B.S.	1968 1984
Valladares	Eduardo Gozon	Philippines	B. Th.	1968
Manglicmot	Eliseo L.	Philippines	B. Th.	1969
Sato	Felicidad	Philippines	B. Th.	1969
Swam	Liem Bian	Indonesia	B. Th.	1969
Cheah	S. Swee Fook	Malaysia	B. Th. M. T.S.	1970 1981
Develos	Betty	Philippines	B.R.E.	1970
Manulid	Reynaldo	Philippines	B. Th. M.A. B.S.	1970 1984
Seleky	Romulus	Indonesia	B. Th.	1970
Ababat	Jose C.	Philippines	B.R.E. B. Th.	1971 1972
Bercero	Felipe Z.	Philippines	B. Th.	1971
Bercero-Balista	Lolita	Philippines	B. Th.	1971
Celeregia	Luis B.	Philippines	B. Th.	1971
Chew	Chee Kim	Malaysia	B. Th.	1971
Dinglas	Rolando.	Philippines	B. Th. M.A. B.S.	1971 1983
Inaray	Meity	Indonesia	B. Th.	1971
Kaious	Kaoru	Marshall Islands	B. Th.	1971
Kim	Chew Chee	Malaysia	B. Th.	1971

Appendix A   131

LAST NAME	FIRST NAME	HOME COUNTRY	DEGREE	YEAR GRANTED
Mailangkay	Piet Hein	Indonesia	B. Th. M.A. B.S.	1971 1984
Monintja	Manuel Edison	Indonesia	B. Th.	1971
Montes	Levi	Philippines	B. Th.	1971
Montes	Rebecca	Philippines	B.R.E.	1971
Rumkeny	Menasse	Indonesia	B. Th. M.A. B.S.	1971 1984
Samson	Anton Loje	Marshall Islands	B. Th.	1971
Sitompul	Saidah	Indonesia	B. Th.	1971
Sarangay	Agustin	Philippines	B. Th.	1972
Basilio	Fernando	Philippines	B. Th. M. Div.	1972 1989
Bongcawil	Perla (Cabajes)	Philippines	B. Th. B.R.E. M.A. B.S.	1972 1978 1988
Lozande	Melba P.	Philippines	B.R.E. B. Th.	1972 1973
Pettyjohn	Arthur	USA	B. Th.	1972
Romero	Danilo R.	Philippines	B. Th. M.A. B.S.	1972 1986
Tibung	Elisa	Philippines	B. Th. B.R.E.	1972 1973
Colar Alvior	Tessie B.	Philippines	B.R.E. B. Th.	1973 1974
Fernandez	Norma	Philippines	B.R.E.	1973
Tagayuna	Estelita A.	Philippines	B. Th.	1973
Abarico	Esterluz	Philippines	B.R.E.	1974
Allen	Crethia U.	Marshall Islands	B. Th. B.R.E.	1974
Balista	Julito	Philippines	B. Th. M.A. B.S.	1974 1985
Bendoy	Thelma	Philippines	B.R.E.	1974
Esteves	Rodulfo P.	Philippines	B.R.E.	1974
Langrine	Neria	Marshall Islands	B. Th. B.R.E.	1974
MacQuinn	Amos	Marshall Islands	B. Th.	1974
Plete	Arturo	Philippines	B.A. B.S. B. Th.	1974 1975
Sobrepena	David	Philippines	B.A. Bib. B. Th.	1974 1975

LAST NAME	FIRST NAME	HOME COUNTRY	DEGREE	YEAR GRANTED
Visca	Abraham C.	Philippines	B. Th. / M.A. B.S.	1974 / 1985
Chan	Kuang Hai Simon	Singapore	B.A. Bib. / B. Th.	1975 / 1976
Cullen	John	Australia	B.A. Bib. / B. Th.	1975 / 1976
Dumanon	Oriel	Philippines	B. Th.	1975
Gutzat	Diethard W.	Australia	B.A. Bib. / B. Th.	1975 / 1976
Musa	Adelaida V.	Philippines	B.R.E. / M.A. C.E.	1975 / 1988
Sasaki	Masaaki	Japan	B.A. Bib. / B. Th.	1975 / 1976
Seruvatu	Akuila	Fiji	B.B.S.	1975
Belizar	Abraham	Philippines	B.B.S.	1976
Abellano	Jordan	Philippines	B.B.S. / M.A. Min. / M. Div.	1976 / 1996 / 1998
An	Byoung Kwan	Korea	B.B.S.	1976
Choi	Ki Poong	Korea	B.A. B.S.	1976
Choi	Kyu Chul	Korea	B.B.S.	1976
Choi	Ki Soon	Korea	B.B.S.	1976
Han	Sang Kook	Korea	B.B.S.	1976
Kim	Seong Do	Korea	B.B.S.	1976
Kim	Chong Nam	Korea	B.A. B.S.	1976
Kim	Chang UK.	Korea	B.A. B.S.	1976
Kim	Won Ju	Korea	B.A. B.S.	1976
Kim	Yong Tae	USA	B.B.S.	1976
Kong	Dong In	Korea	B.A. B.S.	1976
Lee	Kyoung Jae	Korea	B.A. B.S.	1976
Lee	Hong Koo	Korea	B.A. B.S.	1976
Lee	Won Hee	Korea	B.A. B.S.	1976 / 1977
Lee	KwangJi	Korea	B.A. B.S.	1976
Lim	Eui Woong	Korea	B.A. B.S.	1976
Martinez	Demetria	Philippines	B.B.S. / B. Th.	1976 / 1977
Masuecos-Olivo	Bonnie Joy	Philippines	B. R.E.	1976

LAST NAME	FIRST NAME	HOME COUNTRY	DEGREE	YEAR GRANTED
Moon	Jeong Ryul	Korea	B.A. B.S.	1976
Na	Gi Chang	Korea	B.B.S.	1976
Paik	Seung Ho	Korea	B.A. B.S.	1976
Panaguiton	Linda Abay	Philippines	B.R.E. B. Th.	1976
Park	Jung-Keun	Korea	B.B.S.	1976
Seo	Byung Yul	Korea	B.A. B.S.	1976
Shin	Dong Soo	Korea	B.A. B.S.	1976
Tagaya	Tomoko	Japan	B.B.S. B. Th.	1976
Tobing	Micha Natigor Lumba	Indonesia	B.B.S. B. Th.	1976
Visca	Zenaida C.	Philippines	B.R.E.	1976 1977
Anciado	Ric-ces	Philippines	B.B.S.	1977
Bernales	Lydia	Philippines	B.R.E. B. Th.	1977 1978
Cariaso	Felomina C.	Philippines	B.R.E. B. Th.	1977
Cava	Vaciseva R.	Fiji	B.R.E.	1977 1978
Chang	UK Jeong	USA	B.B.S.	1977 1978
Cho	Kyu Seon	Korea	B.B.S.	1977
Digay	Elizabeth	Philippines	B.R.E.	1977
Golbin	Clarita L.	Philippines	B.R.E.	1977
Kim	Chung Soo	Korea	B.A. B.S.	1977
Kim	Min Hee	Korea	B.B.S.	1977
Kunanitu	Aisake	Fiji	B.R.E. M.A. B.S.	1977 1978
Kwon	Boo Hyun	Korea	B.A. B.S.	1977
Lagundi-no-Sibuala	Nelly	Philippines	B.R.E. B. Th.	1977 1985
Lala	Eparama	Fiji	B.A. R.E.	1977 1978
Lesumainai Jalu	Jone	Fiji	B. R.E.	1977 1978
Martinez	Evangeline Lopez	Philippines	B.R.E.	1977
Montajes	Baltazar Jr.	Philippines	B.B.S. B. Th.	1977

LAST NAME	FIRST NAME	HOME COUNTRY	DEGREE	YEAR GRANTED
Nacagilevu	Apakuki Mocelutu	Fiji	B. R.E.	1977 1978
Ortega-Sayson	Beverly M.	Philippines	B.R.E. B. Th.	1977
Paano	Raynaldo	Philippines	B.B.S. M. T.S. B. Th.	1977
Park	Seung Bin	Korea	B.A. R.E.	1977
Rayawa	Josaia	Fiji	B.R.E.	1977 1978 1992 2004
Rosario	Evangelina	Philippines	B.R.E. B. Th.	1977
Sevilla	Demetria Marinez A.	Philippines	B. Th.	1977
Sibuala	Alfonso Sodia	Philippines	B.R.E. B. Th.	1977
Son	Kil Sung	Korea	B.B.S. B. Th.	1977 1986
Taniela	Eroni Raora	Fiji	B.R.E.	1977 1981 1978
Tobing	Elizabeth D.	Indonesia	M.A. Min.	1977
Uelese	Timoteo S.	American Samoa	B.R.E. M.A. B.S.	1977 1978
Wilson	Sande	Philippines	B.R.E. B. Th.	1977
Ylmido	Celina Cortez	Philippines	B.R.E. B. Th.	1977 1978
Caput	Walter T.	Philippines	B.R.E. B. Th. M.A. M. Div.	1978 2004
Abellano	Oral Roberts	Philippines	B.B.S. B. Th.	1978 1979
Atilano	Florida	Philippines	B.B.S.	1978
Cabrillos	Monalisa	Philippines	B.R.E. B. Th.	1978 1980
Chang	Jung	Korea	B.B.S.	1978
Choi	Chang Soo	Korea	B.A. B.S.	1978
Cornelio	Emerita S.	Philippines	B.R.E.	1978
Cornelio	Juan	Philippines	B. Th. B.B.S.	1978

Appendix A 135

LAST NAME	FIRST NAME	HOME COUNTRY	DEGREE	YEAR GRANTED
Espartinas	Simeon J.	Philippines	B.R.E. M.A. C.E.	1978 1985
Gandola	Estelita	Philippines	B.R.E. B. Th.	1978 1980
HalunaJan	Josephine	Philippines	B.R.E.	1978
Ibanez	Juliana	Philippines	B.R.E. M. Div.	1978
Ladura	Merida A.	Philippines	B.R.E. B. Th. M.A. C.E.	1978 1979 1989
Ladura	Segundino	Philippines	B.B.S. B. Th. M.A. B.S.	1978 1979 1989
Langiden	Mely	Philippines	B.R.E.	1978
Lee	Chun Kil	Korea	B.A. B.S.	1978
Raquel	Elizabeth	Philippines	B.R.E. B. Th.	1978 1980
Samonte	Bethoven	Philippines	B.B.S.	1978
Taboclaon	Isidra	Philippines	B.B.S. B. Th.	1978 1979
Tan	Lilia B.	Philippines	B.R.E. M.R.E.	1978 1981
Teh	Betty Bee Tee	Malaysia	B. Th. M.R.E.	1978 1980
Yeang	Yoot Wah	Malaysia	B. Th.	1978
Anaya	Santos	Philippines	B.B.S. M. T.S.	1979 1981
Arangote	Sophia	Philippines	B.R.E. M.A. C.E.	1979
Aung	Myo	Myanmar	B.B.S. M.A. B.S.	1979 1993
Bendoy-Henderson	Wilma	Philippines	B.B.S. M. T.S.	1979 1981
Buyoc	Yolanda	Philippines	B.R.E.	1979
Casaul	Romulo	Philippines	B.B.S.	1979
Dishman	James Daniel	USA	B.B.S.	1979 1992
Estrada	Roxas	Philippines	B.R.E.	1979
Gallego	Dandy V.	Philippines	B.B.S.	1979
Gutierrez	Arlene	Philippines	B.R.E. M.R.E.	1979 1981

LAST NAME	FIRST NAME	HOME COUNTRY	DEGREE	YEAR GRANTED
Hiquiana	Maria Christina	Philippines	B.R.E. M.R.E.	1979 1988
Igualdo	Janet	Philippines	B.B.S.	1979
Lasquite-Barcellano	Rodelyn	Philippines	B.B.S. M. T.S.	1979 1982
Manglicmot	Justino Jr.	Philippines	B.B.S. M.A. Th.	1979 1981
Rioja	Rebecca A.	Philippines	B.R.E.	1979
Sanchez	Patricio	Philippines	B.B.S. B. Th.	1979
Song	Nam Young	Korea	B.A. Bib.	1979
Tabulao	Osias	Philippines	B.B.S.	1979 1982
Yoo	Soon Jong	Korea	B.A. B.S.	1979
Abeysekera	Fred G.	Singapore	B.A. B.S.	1980
Dime	Myrna C.	Philippines	B.B.S.	1980
Engcoy	Lemuel	Philippines	B.B.S. M.A. B.S. M. Div.	1980 1985 1998
Esperanza	Rebecca	Philippines	M.R.E.	1980
Fernandez	Rogelio A.	Philippines	B.B.S.	1980
Kim	Jin Ho	Korea	B.A. B.S.	1980
Latigo	Elda D.	Philippines	B.R.E. M.A. R.E.	1980 1982
Lee	Kang Jae	Korea	B.A. B.S.	1980
Lim	Presentacion	Philippines	B.R.E.	1980
Lolowang	Rudolf Adrian	Indonesia	B.B.S. M. Div.	1980 1983
Novelonio	Renato	Philippines	B.B.S. M.A. B.S.	1980 1991
Pagaialii	Tavita	Samoa	B.B.S. M. T.S. D. Min.	1980 1982 2005
Park	Jae Suk	Korea	B.A. B.S.	1980
Rhee	Kyonng Sup	Korea	B.A. B.S.	1980
Somera	Samuel Gadia	Philippines	B.B.S. B. Th. M.A. B.S.	1980 1981 1985
Tan	Chow May Ling	Singapore	B.B.S. M. T.S.	1980 1982

LAST NAME	FIRST NAME	HOME COUNTRY	DEGREE	YEAR GRANTED
Tan	Chung Liam Derek	Malaysia	B.B.S. M.T.S.	1980 1982
Tandog	Cresencio	Philippines	B.B.S.	1980
Villa	Daniel	Philippines	B.B.S. M. Div.	1980 1983
Artuza	Grace S.	Philippines	B.B.S. M.A. B.S.	1981 1995
Barcellano	Alex C.	Philippines	B.B.S. M.A. B.S.	1981 1983
Cabajes	Tarcelo	Philippines	B.B.S.	1981
Dumanon	Raquel	Philippines	B.B.S.	1981
Ma	Won Suk	Korea	B.B.S. M. Div.	1981 1983
Sayan-Torres	Monica M.	Philippines	M.A. C.E. B.R.E.	1981 1983
Sung	Hsi Sheng Philip	Malaysia	B.B.S. M. Div.	1981 1983
Torres	Alfredo	Philippines	B.A. B.S. M.A. B.S. M. Div.	1981 1982 2003
Alcomendras	Camilo P.	USA	B.A. B.S.	1982
Cagas	Roque, Jr.	Philippines	B.B.S. M. Div.	1982 1983
Ching Phua	Swee Tee Ruth	Malaysia	B.A. B.S. M. Div.	1982 1984
Gaerlan	Elizabeth.	Philippines	B.A. C.E. M.A. C.E.	1982 1983
Italia	Gelita	Philippines	M.A. C.E.	1982
Mendoza	Joel D.	Philippines	B.A. B.S.	1982
Pang	Yan Leng	Singapore	B.A. B.S. M. Div.	1982 1984
Phua Chai Chuan	Anthony	Singapore	B.A. B.S. M. Div.	1982 1983
Verana	Romarico	Philippines	M.A. B.S.	1982
Akraphram	Pradit	Thailand	B.A. B.S.	1983
Almonidovar	Joseph P.	Philippines	B.A. B.S.	1983
An Chin Chih	Ann	Taiwan	B.A. B.S.	1983
Cabantac	Thomas V.	Philippines	B.A. C.E.	1983
Chang	Hyung Sheng (Jacob)	Taiwan	B.A. B.S.	1983
Chen	Chih Chung (Stephen)	Taiwan	B.A. B.S.	1983

LAST NAME	FIRST NAME	HOME COUNTRY	DEGREE	YEAR GRANTED
Chen	Feing Mei (Rebecca)	Taiwan	B.A. B.S.	1983
Chou	Kun Hu (Robert)	Taiwan	B.A. B.S.	1983
Chun	Kiew Ming Dorothy	Malaysia	B.A. B.S.	1983 1987 2016
Esperanza	Daniel B.	Philippines	B.A. B.S. M. Div.	1983
Ezung	E. Nrio	India	M.A. C.E.	1983
Huang	Fu Han	Taiwan	B.A. B.S.	1983
Hung	Joseph Ying-Chuan	Taiwan	B.A. B.S.	1983
Kim	Sun Lae	Korea	M.A. B.S.	1983
Kuo	Chung-Yuan	Taiwan	B.A. B.S.	1983
Ladera	Cecilio C.	Philippines	M.A. B.S.	1983
Lazaro	Samuel	Philippines	B.A. B.S.	1983
Lee Soo Sin	Sharon	Malaysia	B.A. B.S. M.A. Min.	1983
Liew Zoo Yee	Henry	Malaysia	B.A. B.S. M.A. B.S. D. Min.	1983 1994
Lin	Wen Teh	Taiwan	B.A. B.S.	1983
Ma	Jungja Cho, Julie	Korea	B.A. C.E. M.A. C.E.	1983 1986
Tsai	Hui Chiu (Joy)	Taiwan	B.A. B.S.	1983
Tung	Yueh Chun (Esther)	Taiwan	B.A. B.S.	1983
Watanabe	Kihei	Japan	B.A. B.S.	1983
Barrios	Danilo	Philippines	B.A. C.E. M.A. C.E.	1984 1989 1995 2006
Cachola	Joshua A.	Philippines	B.A. B.S. M.A. B.S.	1984 1987
Chen	Andrew Cheng Rung	Taiwan	B.A. B.S.	1984
Cheong	Bertram (K. Hoe)	Singapore	M.A. B.S.	1984 1985
Chiong	Sook Kuen Jenny	Malaysia	B.A. B.S. M.A. B.S. M. Div. D. Min.	1984
Dasalia	Adelaida V.	Philippines	B.A. C.E.	1984
Dayaoen	Tap B.	Philippines	B.A. B.S.	1984

Appendix A 139

LAST NAME	FIRST NAME	HOME COUNTRY	DEGREE	YEAR GRANTED
Foo Kee Chin	Sally	Malaysia	B.A. B.S. M.A. Min.	1984
Foong Chua Kien Ming	Dorothy	Malaysia	B.A. B.S.	1984
Gaco	Johnny C. (Juan Jr.)	Philippines	B.A. B.S.	1984
Guillermo	Angel	Philippines	M.A. B.S. B.A. B.S.	1984
Gulfan	Jeremy Peter	USA	B.A. B.S.	1984
Kang	Tin Yong Albert	Singapore	B.A. B.S. M. Div.	1984
Kim	Eun Chul	Korea	B.A. B.S.	1984
Kok	Chaw Fatt (John)	Malaysia	B.A. B.S.	1984
Ku	Ruth L.H.	Taiwan	B.A. B.S.	1984
LengKong	Josias Leindert	Indonesia	B.A. B.S. M. Div.	1984
Lim	Jeremiah Seng Sik	Singapore	B.A. B.S.	1984 1985
Mariano	Claudio C.	Philippines	M.A. B.S.	1984
Mendoza	Abraham	Philippines	B.A. B.S.	1984
Ng Kim Seng	Benjamin	Malaysia	B.A. B.S. M.A. B.S.	1984
Park	Soon Ja	Korea	B.A. B.S.	1984
Ramaya	Henry K.	Malaysia	B.A. B.S.	1984
Santos	Francisco	Philippines	M.A. B.S.	1984
Tadena	Amalia D.	Philippines	B.A. C.E. M.A. C.E.	1984 1996
Tan Chang Choon	Winston	Singapore	B.A. B.S.	1984
Tse	Haak Mo	Hong Kong	B.A. B.S.	1984
Tubog	Elma Calm	Philippines	M.A. C.E.	1984 1985
Ua-Arreyawan	Panya	Thailand	B.A. B.S.	1984 1985
Vutti Udomlert	Surachai	Thailand	B.A. B.S.	1984
Wichai	Chukiat	Thailand	B.A. B.S.	1984
Bercero	Yolanda B.	Philippines	M.A. C.E.	1985
Cabasag	Virginia A.	Philippines	B.A. B.S.	1985
Chan	Yew Seng Philip	Singapore	B.A. B.S. M.A. B.S.	1985 1988
Chee	Moon Sang	Malaysia	B.A. B.S.	1985

LAST NAME	FIRST NAME	HOME COUNTRY	DEGREE	YEAR GRANTED
Doo	Young Kyoo	Korea	B.A. B.S. M.A. B.S.	1985
Dowdy	Naomi Ruth	Singapore	M.A. B.S.	1985
Ferreros	Harry	Philippines	B.A. B.S. M.A. B.S.	1985 1986
Hartati	Neneng	Indonesia	B.A. C.E.	1985
Ilarde	Joel B.	Philippines	B.A. B.S.	1985
Ko	Phoebe	Taiwan	B.A. B.S.	1985
Lim Cheng Saik	Stanley	Malaysia	B.A. B.S.	1985
Lumahan	Conrado	Philippines	B.A. B.S. M.A. B.S. M. Div. M. Th.	1985 1986 1994 2003
Moses	Dora	Myanmar	B.A. B.S. M. Div.	1985 1986
Park	Jeong Yull	Korea	M.A. Th.	1985
Roslim	Suwandoko	Indonesia	M.A. B.S.	1985
Talatagod	Jaime V.	Philippines	B.A. B.S.	1985
Tan	Simon Gim HockHock	Singapore	M.A. B.S.	1985
Thep Jak	Pramote	Thailand	B.A. C.E. M.A. C.E.	1985 1986
Wong	Yin Ming	Malaysia	B.A. B.S. M.A. B.S.	1985 1991
Yu	Judith Sy	Philippines	B.A. B.S.	1985
Abad Santos	Irineo	Philippines	B.A. B.S. M.A. B.S.	1986 1987
Abbott	William	Philippines	B.A. B.S.	1986
Barroga	Carponio Sr.	Philippines	B.A. B.S.	1986
Baybayan	Consuelo Tamayo	Philippines	M.A. C.E.	1986
Cagas	Gospelaire T.	Philippines	M. Div.	1986
Cetro	Ma Teresa.	Philippines	B.A. B.S. M.A. B.S.	1986 1987
Chan	Chee Wah (Isaac)	Malaysia	B.A. B.S.	1986
Chan	Dominic Weng Flatt.	Malaysia	M.A. B.S. B.A. B.S.	1986 1991
Chen	Hannah Hui Chu	Taiwan	B.A. B.S.	1986
Cheong	Choo (Lydia)	Malaysia	B.A. B.S.	1986
Chua Chong Som	Elisha	Malaysia	B.A. B.S. M.A. Min.	1986 1994
De Leon	Victorina	Philippines	B.A. C.E.	1986

Appendix A

LAST NAME	FIRST NAME	HOME COUNTRY	DEGREE	YEAR GRANTED
Estrada	Joseph N.	Philippines	M.A. B.S.	1986
Farase	Jane G.	Philippines	M.A. C.E.	1986
Guevara	Oral Paul	Philippines	B.A. B.S. M.A. B.S.	1986
Hardie	Adam	Scotland	M.A. B.S.	1986
Kim	Byung Yoon	Korea	B.A. B.S.	1986
Kowit	Kaeokhoomprai	Thailand	B.A. B.S.	1986
Lee	Jonathan M. D.	Taiwan	B.A. B.S.	1986 1987
Lezada	Rachel	Philippines	B.A. B.S. M. Div.	1986 1987
Liao	Sarah P.	Philippines	B.A. C.E.	1986
Lim	Glen Cheng Huat	Singapore	B.A. B.S. M.A. B.S.	1986 1994
Lim Ah Heok	Margaret	Singapore	B.A. B.S.	1986
Lim Ah Mui	Jean	Singapore	B.A. C.E. M.A. C.E.	1986 1992
Molina	Ernesto	Philippines	B.A. B.S. M.A.	1986 1988
Mow Sai Fong	Betty	Singapore	B.A. B.S.	1986
Ng	Kok Kee (Richard)	Malaysia	B.A. B.S.	1986
Niumataiwalu	Sepesa	Fiji	M.A. B.S.	1986
Ong	Caleb Y.H.	Taiwan	B.A. B.S.	1986 1989
Prasert	Tepjuk	Thailand	B.A. B.S.	1986
Pratheepthin-thong	Malee	Thailand	B.A. B.S. M. Div.	1986
Quek Jwee Leng	Edwin	Singapore	M.A. B.S.	1986
Rajendran	Elijah	Malaysia	B.A. B.S.	1986
Sargent	Timothy	England	B.A. B.S.	1986
Sato	Akio	Japan	B.A. B.S.	1986
Sinnadurai	Terrence Kok	Malaysia	B.A. B.S.	1986
Soh	Bee Khim	Singapore	B.A. B.S.	1986
Tamayo	Baybayan Consuelo	Philippines	M.A. C.E.	1986
Tham	Ton Hing	Malaysia	B.A. B.S.	1986
Wilson	Lydia B.	Philippines	M.A. B.S.	1986
Aihara	Kenji	Japan	B.A. B.S.	1987 1996

LAST NAME	FIRST NAME	HOME COUNTRY	DEGREE	YEAR GRANTED
Arianayagam	Indranie	Malaysia	B.A. B.S.	1987
Cappal	Heredel P.	Philippines	M.A. B.S.	1987 1989
Ceniza	Helen B.	Philippines	B.A. C.E. M.A. C.E. M. Div.	1987
Chan	Ping Onn (Luke)	Malaysia	B.A. B.S.	1987 1989
Chee Yeow Seng	David	Singapore	B.A. B.S. M.A. B.S.	1987
Cheng	Yi Lin	Hong Kong	B.A. B.S.	1987 1988 1990
Chin	Choong Tet Ronnie	Malaysia	B.A. B.S.	1987
Chin	Yoon Lee Lisa	Malaysia	B.A. B.S.	1987
Chua Kuan Wee	Lawrence	Singapore	B.A. B.S.	1987
Co (Chua)	Rosa	Philippines	M.A. B.S.	1987
Cuasito	Elisha C.	Philippines	B.A. B.S.	1987
Divino	Angeles C.	Philippines	B.A. C.E.	1987
Go Lee Kian	Katherine	Malaysia	B.A. B.S.	1987
Ibanez	Nena	Philippines	M.A. C.E.	1987
Ibanez	Nelly	Philippines	M.A. C.E. M. Div.	1987
Lausa	Fernando	Philippines	B.A. B.S. M.A. B.S.	1987 1988
Leasau	Silas J.	American Samoa	B.A. B.S.	1987 2002
Lezada	John Fajardo	Philippines	B.A. B.S. M.A. B.S.	1987 1988 1990
Lim	Jong Hong Feztus	Singapore	B.A. B.S.	1987
Lim Choon Hong	Deborah	Singapore	B.A. B.S.	1987
Lin Ch'un Hsiung	James	Taiwan	B.A. B.S.	1987
Loo	Hock Seng Benjamin	Singapore	M.A. B.S. M.A. C.E.	1987
Loo	Irene Chiou	Singapore	B.A. C.E. M.A. C.E. M.A. B.S.	1987 1989

Appendix A 143

LAST NAME	FIRST NAME	HOME COUNTRY	DEGREE	YEAR GRANTED
Mah Mei Kuen	Hephzibah	Thailand	B.A. C.E. M.A. C.E.	1987 1988
Mothanaprakoon	Ezra	Thailand	B.A. B.S. M. Div.	1987
Nana	Dionisio C.	Philippines	B.A. B.S. M.A. B.S.	1987 1989
Ng Kong Chiew	Casey	Singapore	B.A. B.S. M. Div.	1987
Ng Mei Lin	Grace	Malaysia	B.A. B.S.	1987
Nulud	Gerardo Tan	Philippines	M.A. B.S.	1987
Ong	Hock Hye (Peter)	Malaysia	B.A. B.S.	1987 1989
Ong Kin Kin	Winnie Wong	Singapore	B.A. B.S. M.A. B.S.	1987 1998
Pang	Ek Kwan	Singapore	B.A. B.S.	1987 2001
Pantig	Thelma R.	Philippines	B.A. C.E.	1987
Roengsang	Sathaan	Thailand	B.A. B.S.	1987
Samson	Edilberto D.	Philippines	M.A. B.S. M. Div.	1987
Seow Bee Lian	Maureen	Singapore	B.A. B.S. M.A. B.S.	1987 1989
Seow Kuan Yong	Lawrence	Singapore	B.A. B.S. M.A. B.S.	1987 1991
Sim	Lee Cheng, Eileen	Singapore	B.A. B.S.	1987
Soh Hui Leng	Davina	Singapore	B.A. B.S. M. Div.	1987 1994
Suico	Joseph Rommel	Philippines	M. Div. Th. M.	1987 1989
Tio Swee Cheng	Madeline	Singapore	M.A. B.S.	1987
Uchimura	Tamotsu	Japan	M.A. B.S. M. Div.	1987
Yeoh Teng Beng	Benjamin	Malaysia	M.A. Min. B.A. B.S.	1987
Yong Ah Mui	Jean	Singapore	M.A. C.E.	1987
Yoshino	Seiichiro	Japan	B.A. B.S.	1987
Acena	Felipe	Philippines	M.A. B.S.	1988
Adhikary	Ajoy	India	M.A. B.S.	1988
Annadorai	George	Singapore	M.A. B.S.	1988

LAST NAME	FIRST NAME	HOME COUNTRY	DEGREE	YEAR GRANTED
Castillo	Elena Roque	Philippines	M.A. B.S.	1988
Castromayor	Gaudencio	Philippines	M.A. C.E.	1988
Chan	Jong Hwa	Korea	B.A. B.S.	1988
Cher Lian Chye	Roland Kester	Singapore	B.A. B.S.	1988
Cho	Byung Kwan	Korea	B.A. B.S.	1988
Galangga	Magdalena S.	Philippines	M.A. C.E.	1988
Getgaew	Chalearm	Thailand	B.A. B.S M. Div. D.Min	1988
Goh Khoon Chew	Jason	Malaysia	B.A. B.S.	1988
Jan	King Hoon (Roy)	Malaysia	B.A. B.S. M.A.	1988
Jeong	Jae Yong	Korea	B.A. B.S.	1988
Jeong	Chi Eel	Korea	B.A. B.S. M. Div.	1988
Jeong	Duk-Man	Korea	B.A. B.S.	1988
Kang	Sung Man	Korea	B.A. B.S.	1988 1993
Kho	Tuk Hunt (Eric)	Malaysia	B.A. B.S.	1988
Kim	So Young	Korea	B.A. C.E.	1988
Kim	Jong-guk	Korea	B.A. C.E. M. Div. D. Min.	1988
Kim	Byung Ho	Korea	B.A. B.S.	1988
Koo Teik Huat	Eric	Malaysia	B.A. B.S.	1988
Kunagar	Buppa	Thailand	B.A. B.S.	1988
Lagundino	Esaias	Philippines	B.A. B.S.	1988
Lee	Foong Ling	Malaysia	B.A. B.S.	1988
Lee	Sam Yong	Korea	B.A. B.S.	1988
Malinis	Theresa Alma F.	Philippines	M.A. B.S.	1988 1989
Orencio	Stanley C.	Philippines	B.A. B.S.	1988 1989
Ow	Chong Kheng (Stanley)	Singapore	B.A. B.S.	1988
Praimat	Jumporn	Thailand	B.A. B.S.	1988
Rimba	Hariagus	Indonesia	M. Div.	1988
Ronghanam	Buakab	Thailand	B.A. B.S.	1988

LAST NAME	FIRST NAME	HOME COUNTRY	DEGREE	YEAR GRANTED
Samerjai	Srimala	Thailand	B.A. B.S.	1988 1992 2015
Seduagchai	Surasak	Thailand	B.A. B.S.	1988
Siew	Kin Wai Arie	Malaysia	B.A. B.S.	1988
Sutcliffe	Peter A.	Australia	M.A. B.S. M.A. Th.	1988 1990
Thomas	Erna	Philippines	M.A. C.E.	1988 1990
Tiapson	Pedro Jr.	Philippines	M.A. B.S. M. Div.	1988
Uchimura	Naoko	Japan	B.A. C.E. M.A. C.E.	1988 1991 2006
Whungkhum	Noppadol	Thailand	B.A. B.S.	1988
Wibrata	I Dewa Gede Alit	Indonesia	M.A. B.S.	1988
Chan	Nam Chen	Malaysia	B.A. B.S.	1989
Chen	Esther Chia-Rung	Taiwan	B.A. B.S.	1989
Chia	Beng Hock	Singapore	M.A. B.S. D. Min.	1989
Cho	Byoung Kee	Australia	B.B.S.	1989
Espiritu	Daniel	Philippines	M. Div.	1989
Gadallo	Pepito T.	Philippines	M.A. B.S.	1989
Ho Mun Sang	Michael	Malaysia	B.A. B.S.	1989
Jeong	Young Mee	Korea	B.A. C.E. M.A. C.E.	1989
Leung	Wai Man	Hong Kong	M.A. B.S. M. Div. D. Min.	1989
Leung	Josephine	Philippines	M.A. B.S. M. Div.	1989
Lim Ortega	Racquel	England	M. Div.	1989
Madarang	Jerome	Philippines	M.A. B.S.	1989 1999 2006
Munoz	Leo M.	Philippines	M.A. B.S.	1989 2000
Ong Duen Yih	Richard	Malaysia	B.A. B.S.	1989
Salarda	Ernesto S.	Philippines	M.A. B.S.	1989 2000

LAST NAME	FIRST NAME	HOME COUNTRY	DEGREE	YEAR GRANTED
Sarkar	Arun Kumar	India	M. Div.	1989
Sim Cheng Neo	Diana	Singapore	B.A. B.S. M.A. B.S.	1989
Tan	Pek Har	Malaysia	M.A. C.E.	1989
Tan	King Hoon/Roy	Malaysia	B.A.B.S. M.A.	1989 1994
Taylor	Nannie	Malaysia	M.A. B.S.	1989
Tsai	Joseph Cheng Ting	Taiwan	B.A. B.S.	1989
Tsai	Stephen Shou-Ch'eng	Taiwan	B.A. B.S.	1989
Wall	James Norman	USA	M.A. B.S.	1989 1990
Wee	Woon Teck	Singapore	M.A. B.S.	1989
Wichitnantana	Anuparp	Thailand	M.A. B.S.	1989 1990
Wu Kwong Piu	Nicholas	Malaysia	M.A. B.S.	1989
Yap Thin Yoon	Kelly	Singapore	B.A. B.S.	1989
Yeo Hook Leng	Alfred	Singapore	B.A. B.S.	1989
Banner	Algernon	Fiji	M.A. B.S.	1990
Benedictus	Robert	Indonesia	M.A.	1990
Budiyono	Gatut	Indonesia	M. Div. D. Min.	1990
Bundang	Jacinto E.	Philippines	M.A. B.S. M. Div.	1990
Chan	Dahlia Maylin	Thailand	B.A. B.S.	1990
Chatudomkul	Soraya	Thailand	B.A. B.S.	1990
Chou	Chun Chun (Jenny)	Taiwan	B.A. B.S.	1990
dela Cruz	Roli	Philippines	M. Div.	1990
Foo Chaw Sou	Bernard	Singapore	B.A. B.S.	1990
Fuentes	Alex	Philippines	M.A. B.S. M. Div. D. Min.	1990 2001 2007
Goh Chye Choo	Douglas	Singapore	M.A. B.S.	1990
Kim	Esther	USA	M.A. B.S.	1990 2001 2007
Kong Kin Thew	Tommy	Malaysia	M.A. B.S.	1990
Liu Kuei-tzu	Eunice	Taiwan	B.A. B.S.	1990
Misael	Alan	Philippines	M.A. B.S. M. Div.	1990 2006

Appendix A 147

LAST NAME	FIRST NAME	HOME COUNTRY	DEGREE	YEAR GRANTED
Ng Tech Lee	Frankie	Singapore	M. Div.	1990
Okafor	Reuben C.	Nigeria	M.A. B.S.	1990
Pelias-Fredeluces	Sarah	Philippines	M.A. C.E.	1990
Peng Hsin-Ren	Victor	Taiwan	B.A. B.S.	1990 2006
Pepito	Amelia	Philippines	M.A. B.S.	1990
Rarama	Danilo	Philippines	M.A. B.S.	1990 2003
Ricaborda	Maximo	Philippines	B.A. B.S.	1990 2001 2007
Saengkhoontod	Mualrerdee	Thailand	M.A. C.E.	1990
Saengkhoontod	Tanapong	Thailand	M.A.	1990
Seow Kah Sin	George	Singapore	M.A. B.S. B.A. B.S.	1990
Tay Boon Hui	Alan	Singapore	B.A. B.S.	1990
Vela	Peter K.	Malaysia	B.A. B.S. M.A. M. Div.	1990 2006
Wee Lian Kim	Katherine	Malaysia	B.A. B.S.	1990
Won	Jong Bum	Korea	M.A. B.S.	1990
Beaumont	Stephen	Australia	M.A.	1991
Belono-ac	Melchor	Philippines	M. Div.	1991
Chua Boon Leng	Roderick	Singapore	M.A. B.S.	1991
Dionson	Noel	Philippines	M. Div.	1991
Erojo	Jerry	Philippines	M. Div.	1991
Gani	Desmond	Fiji	M. Div.	1991
Hall	Stuart	Australia	M.A. Th.	1991
Hau	Lun Cing (Mary)	Myanmar	M. Div.	1991
Hong	Chelee Gi	Korea	M. Div.	1991
Inkeaw	Thonglek	Thailand	B.A. B.S.	1991
Jaro	Danilo N.	Philippines	M.A.	1991
Khai	Swan Go	Myanmar	M. Div.	1991
Kham	Hau Lian	Myanmar	M. Div. Th. M.	1991 1994
Kim	Charles Kook	USA	M.A. Th.	1991
Lacay	Theodora	Philippines	M.A. C.E.	1991

LAST NAME	FIRST NAME	HOME COUNTRY	DEGREE	YEAR GRANTED
Lam	Norma June	Malaysia	M.A. M. Div. Th. M. D. Min	1991 1995 1995 1998
Lim	Yeu Chuen	Malaysia	M.A. D. Min.	1991 2014
Lim	Seng Giap Michael	Singapore	M. Div.	1991
Lye	Norma J.	Malaysia	M. Div.	1991
Niog	Herson A	Philippines	M.A.	1991
Pambid Caezar	Paul C.	Philippines	M.A.	1991
Rosal	Marbelito T.	Philippines	M.A. M. Div.	1991 1993
Santonia	Arnold L.	Philippines	M.A. M. Div.	1991 1993
Soabas	Emmanuel	Philippines	M.A.	1991
Tan Seow Wei	Joanna	Malaysia	M.A. M. Div.	1991 1992
Verana	Maria Cecilia	Philippines	M.A. M. Div.	1991 1992
Wutti-Udomlert	Puangtong	Thailand	B.A. B.S.	1991
Arumainayagam	Lawrence	India	M. Div.	1992
Cabangangan	Josefa	Philippines	M.A. M. Div.	1992 1994
Chan	K. George	Singapore	M.A. B.S.	1992
Chee Siew Tai	Suen	Malaysia	B.A. B.S.	1992
Chongchansito	Pasuk	Thailand	B.A. B.S.	1992
Eguia	Joselito N.	Philippines	M. Div.	1992
Fave	Emmanuel	Papua New Guinea	M.A. Th.	1992
Filson	William	Australia	M.A. M. Div. D. Min.	1992 1993 2006
Hunt	David	Australia	M. Div.	1992
Jeong	Chi Young	Korea	M. Div.	1992
Khor	Eng Lian	Malaysia	B.A. B.S.	1992
Koh	Joo Fung	Malaysia	B.A. B.S. M.A. Min.	1992 1999
Lian	Gin Za	Myanmar	M. Div.	1992
Lodevico	Melecio A.	Philippines	M.A.	1992
Phoon	Kum Yew	Malaysia	M. Div.	1992

Appendix A 149

LAST NAME	FIRST NAME	HOME COUNTRY	DEGREE	YEAR GRANTED
Ponce	Manolo S.	Philippines	M.A. Th.	1992
Sangsawang-sajjakul	Sommai	Thailand	B.A. B.S.	1992
Sato	Joanna	Malaysia	M. Div.	1992
Sato	Yoichi	Japan	M. Div.	1992
Smith	Ross N.	Australia	M.A.	1992
Solano	Reynaldo	Philippines	M.A. M. Div.	1992 1993
Tai	Ai Theng Tony	Singapore	M.A. B.S.	1992
Ting	Chiew Yee	Malaysia	M. Div.	1992
Waqa	Josefa	Fiji	M. Div.	1992
Wongsansern	Wiwien	Thailand	B.A. B.S.	1992
Abeysekera	Rita L.	Singapore	B.A. B.S.	1993
Asuncion	Jobert	Philippines	M.A. Min.	1993
Catipon	Leonora A.	Philippines	M. Div.	1993
Chin K. Fatt	Laurence	Singapore	M.A.	1993
Choe	Soo Il	Korea	M.A.	1993
Choi	Eun Joo	Korea	M.A. Th.	1993
Ducayag	Shirley	Philippines	M.A. Min.	1993
Garcia	Leonilo	Philippines	M.A. Th.	1993
Hoe Swee Yoke	Rosalind	Malaysia	M.A.	1993
Kelly	David S.	USA	M.A. Min.	1993
Khoo	Bee Lian (Linda)	Malaysia	B.A. B.S.	1993
Lagman	Olivia (Kisaki)	Philippines	M.A. M. Div.	1993 1995
Lee	Sang Yong	Korea	M. Div.	1993
Lian	Qui Lin	Malaysia	M.A. B.S.	1993
Liau Kok Wah	Michael	Malaysia	M.A. B.S.	1993
Limanta	Indrijanti	Indonesia	M. Div.	1993
Octaviano	Jerry P.	Philippines	M.A.	1993
Ooi Kok Soon	Roland	Malaysia	M.A.	1993
Opena	Juan R.	Philippines	M.A.	1993
Park	Jong-Seung	Korea	B.A. B.S.	1993
Reyes	Rolando R.	Philippines	M.A.	1993
Sainz	John B.	Philippines	M.A.	1993
Seo	In Kim	Korea	M. Div.	1993

LAST NAME	FIRST NAME	HOME COUNTRY	DEGREE	YEAR GRANTED
Seo	Jeong Seok	Korea	M.A. Th.	1993
Setiawan	Budi	Indonesia	M. Div.	1993
Tan Nam Hoon	Nancy	Singapore	M.A.	1993
Tan Pooi Ik	Marcus	Malaysia	B.A. B.S.	1993
Tasker	Craig L.	Australia	M. Div.	1993
Teo Lam Hong	Grace	Singapore	M.A. B.S.	1993
Wiratno	Paulus	Indonesia	M. Div.	1993
Yap	Marlene Y.	Philippines	M.A. M. Div.	1993 1998
Yeol	Yoon Jeong	Korea	M. Div.	1993
Balista	Gunder S.	Philippines	M.A.	1994
Casas	Xerxes L.	Philippines	M. Div.	1994
Chan Abay	Robert	Myanmar	M.A. Th. M.A. Min.	1994
Claudio	Juan B. Jr.	Philippines	M.A. Min.	1994 1995
Foo	Moy Peng	Malaysia	M.A. Min.	1994
Francis	Edward	India	M. Th.	1994
Friend	John Allan	Australia	M.A.	1994
Hao	Marleen L.	Philippines	M.A.	1994
Horst	John	USA	M.A.	1994
Kim	Cheol Ung	Korea	M.A. Th.	1994
Kim	Jin-Kyu	Korea	M. Div.	1994
Kim To Chik	Paul	Malaysia	M. Div.	1994
Ladera	Adelina	Philippines	M.A. Min. M. Div. D. Min.	1994
Lee	Chooi Luen	Malaysia	M. Div.	1994
Lee Siew Ming	Calvin	Singapore	M.A.	1994
Lim Ngee Hui	Brenda	Singapore	M.A.	1994
Liu	Chih Chan	Taiwan	M.A. Min.	1994
Lua	Fernando	Philippines	M.A. Th.	1994
Magbilang-Llamera	Naomi A.	Philippines	M.A.	1994
Ong Chuan Leong	Andrew	Singapore	M.A.	1994
Pak Cheong Huat	Christopher	Malaysia	M.A.	1994

LAST NAME	FIRST NAME	HOME COUNTRY	DEGREE	YEAR GRANTED
Park	Jeong Su	Korea	M.A.	1994
Peran	Israel E.	Philippines	M.A. Min.	1994
Reiher	James K.	Australia	M.A. Th.	1994
Saipani	Terry	American Samoa	M.A. Min.	1994
Sendiong	Lourdes	Philippines	M.A. Th.	1994
Tam Hing Kau	Joshua	Hong Kong	M.A. B.S.	1994
Towner	John C.	Australia	M.A. Th.	1994
Vakasausau	Viliame	Fiji	M.A. M. Div.	1994
Wang Lin Shang	Nellia Chan	Malaysia	B.A. B.S.	1994 1996 2007
Yeap Kam Foo	David	Malaysia	M.A. B.S.	1994 1995
Ahle	James P.	USA	M.A. Min.	1995
Cariño	Joyce N.	Philippines	M.A. Min.	1995
Chin	Pauline Lai Imm.	Malaysia	M. Div.	1995
Choi	Sung Woon	Korea	M. Div.	1995
Chuleerak	Werasak	Thailand	B.A. B.S.	1995
Fountain	Allison Kay	New Zealand	M. Div.	1995
Fuentes	Julie C.	Philippines	M.A. Min.	1995
Ithivech	Boochai	Thailand	B.A. B.S.	1995
Jeon	Sun-Hueng	Korea	M. Div.	1995
Khiew	Sak Joon (Jackson)	Malaysia	M.A. M. Div.	1995 1996
Kwek	Sew Kian	Singapore	M.A. Th. M. Div.	1995 1998
Lee	Yong Nam	Korea	M.A.	1995
Loh Tai Kan	James	Malaysia	M.A. Min.	1995
Margallo	Reynaldo B.	Philippines	M.A. Th. M. Div.	1995
Miranda	David B.	Philippines	M. Div.	1995
Nagamuthu	John	Malaysia	M.A. B.S.	1995
Nartatez	Edgar Rene	Philippines	M.A. Th.	1995
Panpadungkul	Patchanee	Thailand	B.A. B.S.	1995
Passakorn	Baina	Thailand	B.A. B.S.	1995
Peerasthien	Vicha	Thailand	B.A. B.S.	1995
Phupan	Kajohn	Thailand	B.A. B.S.	1995

LAST NAME	FIRST NAME	HOME COUNTRY	DEGREE	YEAR GRANTED
Pimpun	Yongyut	Thailand	B.A. B.S.	1995
Pramkaew	Chittra	Thailand	B.A. B.S.	1995
Quah Peng San	Jason	Malaysia	M.A. Th.	1995
Raguingan	Samuel	Philippines	M.A. / M. Div.	1995 / 1996
Sanmuang	Samak	Thailand	B.A. B.S.	1995
Silagan	Anesia T.	Philippines	M.A. Min.	1995
Srisomboon	Kumpon	Thailand	B.A. B.S.	1995
Tejano	Wilfred S.	Philippines	M. Div.	1995
Thang	Sian Cin	Myanmar	M.A. Min.	1995
Thungprer	Kritsada	Thailand	B.A. B.S.	1995
Wilks	Ralph B.	USA	M. Div.	1995 / 1999
Wongsida	Bunroeng	Thailand	B.A. B.S.	1995
Balbuena	Jeremiah	Philippines	M.A.	1996
Carter	Steven	USA	M.A. Min. / M. Div.	1996 / 1997
Cho	Young Mo	Korea	M. Div.	1996
Cortez	Imelda D.	Philippines	M.A. Min.	1996
Delfin	Jessie Sunday	Philippines	B.A. B.S.	1996
Finau	Sateki	Tonga	M.A. Min.	1996
Guevara	Jerry	Philippines	M.A. Min. / M. Div.	1996
Herrera	Rodel G.	Philippines	M.A. Min.	1996
Jang	Kwang Jin	Korea	M. Div.	1996
Kaisau	Semiti	Fiji	M.A.	1996
Kim	Gyun Hee	Korea	M.A. Min.	1996
Kim	Hyun Young	Philippines	M.A. Min.	1996
Lumibao	Sonny A.	Philippines	M.A. Th.	1996
Pardede	Hudus	Indonesia	M. Div.	1996
Ramanayake	Don Upali	Sri Lanka	M.A.	1996
Ramli	Milka	Indonesia	M. Div.	1996
Rody	Michael E.	USA	M.A. Min. / M. Div.	1996 / 1997
Sim Ah Geok	Eileen	Malaysia	M.A. Min.	1996 / 2004
Sinel	Elvita R.	Philippines	M.A. Min.	1996

Appendix A 153

LAST NAME	FIRST NAME	HOME COUNTRY	DEGREE	YEAR GRANTED
Suico	Laulhati	Philippines	M.A. Min.	1996
Tempornsatien	Surasit	Thailand	M. Div.	1996
Vicente	John	Philippines	M.A. Min.	1996
Yap Boon Kien	Rocky	Malaysia	M.A. Min.	1996
Yee	Tham Wan	Malaysia	M.A. Min. M. Th.	1996
Agengo	Elly Ayieko	Kenya	M.A. Min. M. Div.	1997
Baek	Seung Hwan	Korea	M. Div.	1997
Baobaoen	Florentina S.	Philippines	M.A. Min.	1997
Houger	Weldyn Beryl	USA	M.A. Min.	1997
Igualdo-Gaiwen	Belina C.	Philippines	M.A. Min.	1997
Kang	Jae Koo	Korea	M.A. Th. M. Div.	1997
Kathiripillai	Sinnadurai T.	Malaysia	M.A. Min.	1997
Kim	Suk Kyu	Korea	B.A. B.S.	1997
Kurene	Faalolo	Samoa	M.A. Th. M. Div.	1997
Loke	King Cheong	Malaysia	M.A. Th.	1997
Nam	Myeong Shin	Korea	M. Div.	1997
Park	Won Il	Korea	M.A. Th.	1997 1998
Pecsoy	Jerry	Philippines	M. Div.	1997
Pineda	Lloyd C.	Philippines	M.A. Min.	1997
Ro	Deog Myeong	Korea	M.A. Min. M. Div.	1997
Soerono	Samuel?	Indonesia	M. Div.	1997
Tai Lee Cheng	Rosalind	Malaysia	M.A. Th. M. Div.	1997
Teh Ooi Heng	Julia	Malaysia	M.A. Th. M. Div.	1997 1998
Thanju	Mahesh P.	Nepal	M. Div.	1997 2006
Thio	Lillian	Singapore	M.A. Th.	1997
Wiyono	Gani	Indonesia	M.A. Th. M. Th.	1997
Walker	Susan Maree	Australia	M.A. Min. M. Div.	1998 2001
Chelliah	Irangani G.	Sri Lanka	M.A. Min.	1998
Cheng	William So	Philippines	M. Div.	1998

LAST NAME	FIRST NAME	HOME COUNTRY	DEGREE	YEAR GRANTED
Chia Siew Lian	Anita	Singapore	M. Div.	1998
Engcoy	Dynice Rosanny	Philippines	M.A. Min. M. Div.	1998 2003
Filson	Gayle	Australia	M.A. Min.	1998
Gamboa	Bienvenido	Philippines	M.A. Min. M. Div.	1998 2010
Jang	Woon Kyong	Korea	M.A. Min. M. Div.	1998 1999
Kisaki	Tom	Japan	M. Div.	1998
Mulyanto	Antonius	Indonesia	M.A. Min.	1998
Pacleb	Angelita T.	Philippines	M.A. Min.	1998
Paul	Zia	Pakistan	M.A. Min. M. Div.	1998 2000
Shota	Sterling	USA	M. Div.	1998
Wada	Keiji	Japan	M.A. Min. M. Div.	1998 1999
Aipolo	Sitiveni Graham (Steve)	Tonga	M.A. Min. M. Div.	1999
Arslan	Otgontseteg	Mongolia	M.A. Th. M. Div.	1999 2000
Asban	Benedicto	Philippines	M.A. Min.	1999
Ayurzana	Baatar	Mongolia	M.A. Min.	1999
Beh	Chung Heng	Malaysia	M.A. Min.	1999
Bono	Michael	Papua New Guinea	M.A. Th.	1999
Boseman	Fabiola	Philippines	Grad. Cert. M. Div.	1999 2001
Buri	Bernard	Papua New Guinea	M.A. Th. M. Div.	1999 2002
Capapas	Wenifredo	Philippines	M.A. Miss.	1999
Chan	Poh Yin, Connie	Malaysia	M.A. Min.	1999
Chung	Jung Mo	Korea	M.A. Th. M. Div.	1999 2001 2011
Codangos	Jack	Philippines	M.A. Min.	1999
Cole	Harold	USA	M.A. Miss.	1999
Davaadar	Togtohk-Ulzii	Mongolia	M.A. Th. M. Div.	1999
Doyle-Davidson	Veronica	Great Britain	M.A. Th.	1999
Esteva	Rebecca	Philippines	M.A. Min.	1999

Appendix A 155

LAST NAME	FIRST NAME	HOME COUNTRY	DEGREE	YEAR GRANTED
Hazard	Jenny Lee	Taiwan	M.A. Min.	1999
Hazard	Wayne	USA	M.A. Min.	1999
Jung	Ki Yang	Korea	M.A. Miss.	1999
Kim	Seong Tae	Korea	M. Div.	1999
Kim	Jin Oh	Korea	M.A. Min. M. Div.	1999 2006 2016
Lai Yueh Chi	Joyce	Taiwan	M.A. Min.	1999 2000
Lamjav	Soyolmaa	Mongolia	M.A. Min.	1999
Leong Sek Chuen	Daniel	Malaysia	M.A. Min.	1999
Lim	Amelia	Philippines	M.A. Min.	1999
Loh Kok Wah	Daniel	Malaysia	M.A. Min.	1999
Mang	Kham Khen	Myanmar	M. Div.	1999
Mongas	Paulino Jr.	Philippines	M.A. Min.	1999
Murray	Peter Gerard	Malaysia	M.A. Min.	1999
Nagasawa	Makito	Japan	M.A. Th. M. Div.	1999 2007
Ng Bee Lian	Magdalene	Singapore	M.A. Th.	1999
Ng Teng Beng	Samuel	Malaysia	M.A. Min.	1999
Oh	Sang Hoon	Korea	M.A. Min. M. Div. D. Min.	1999
Pack	Jung Hee	Korea	Grad. Cert.	1999 2011
Palpal-latoc	Danilo	Philippines	Grad. Cert.	1999
Park	Doo Won	Korea	M. Div.	1999
Poore	Nesarani (Esther)	Malaysia	M.A. Min.	1999
Remojo	Delia	Philippines	M. Div.	1999
Saw	Tint San Oo	Myanmar	M. Div. M. Th. Ph. D	1999 2001 2011
Sheng	Yen Cheng/Catherine	Malaysia	M.A. Min.	1999
Tan	Yong Heng	Malaysia	M.A. Min.	1999
Tay	Hey Tong	Singapore	M.A. Min.	1999
Teh	Siew Lian (Florence)	Malaysia	M.A. Min.	1999

LAST NAME	FIRST NAME	HOME COUNTRY	DEGREE	YEAR GRANTED
Tejedo	Joel	Philippines	M.A. Min. M. Div. D. Min.	1999 2007 2011
Vueta	Penaia Raika Neori	Fiji	M.A. Min.	1999
Wan	Lai Meng	Singapore	M.A. Theo.	1999
Wilks	Melany	USA	M.A. Th.	1999
Yao	Sik Thi (John)	Australia	M.A. Min.	1999 2011
Yun Chee Kong	Richard	Malaysia	M.A. Min.	1999
Boucher	Linda	Philippines	Grad. Cert. M. Div.	2000 2001
Catanes	Mayo	Philippines	M.A. Min. M. Div.	2000 2001
Chua	Pui Bak Tony	Malaysia	M. Div.	2000
Colley/Henry	Nina	USA	M.A. Miss.	2000 2001
Coz	Prudencio	Philippines	M.A. Min. M. Div. D. Min.	2000 2002 2020
Dawagui/ Buri	Yolanda	Philippines	M. Div.	2000
dela Cruz	Barbara	Philippines	M.A. Min.	2000
Dionson	Alan Paul	Philippines	M.A. Min.	2000
Duong	Huu Duc	Vietnam	M. Min. M. Div.	2000
Ensalada	Adrian	Philippines	M.A. Min.	2000
Hilsinger	David Ray	USA	M.A. Min.	2000 2008
Kham	Cin Khen	Myanmar	M.A. Min. M. Div.	2000
Kitchens	Christopher Sean	USA	M.A. Th.	2000
Koizumi	Satoshi	Japan	M. Div.	2000
Koizumi	Misako	Japan	M.A. Th.	2000
Kusu	Megumi	Japan	M. Div.	2000
Lee	Foh Fatt (David)	Singapore	M.A. Min.	2000
Leong	Wai Fun	Malaysia	M.A. Min.	2000
Lim	Ah Ching (Cecilia)	Malaysia	M.A. Min.	2000
Ling	Soon Yuen	Malaysia	M.A. Min.	2000
Lolopua	Edgell Spangler	Vanuatu	M.A. Th.	2000 2002

Appendix A 157

LAST NAME	FIRST NAME	HOME COUNTRY	DEGREE	YEAR GRANTED
Longheta	Robert Lal	Myanmar	M. Div.	2000
Luliano	John	Australia	M. Min.	2000
Madhavan	Sheal Shadra	Fiji	M.A. Min.	2000
Marsch	Dorothee	Germany	M.A. Min.	2000
Martin	Randall Dale	Indonesia	M.A. Min.	2000
McIntyre	Simon	Australia	M. Div.	2000
Moralizon	Galileo J.	Philippines	M. Div.	2000
Multi	Arif	Indonesia	M. Div.	2000
Paciteng	Jose	Philippines	M.A. Min.	2000
Reyes	Erlinda	Philippines	M. Div. M. Th.	2000
Soh	Yoke Siew (Alexander)	Malaysia	M.A. Min.	2000
Somera	Minaflor	Philippines	M.A. Min. M. Div	2000 2002
Strange	Kendra lynette	USA	M.A Th.	2000
Suguta	Aloesi Bolakoro	Fiji	M.A. Min.	2000
Tan	Thuan Loy Alfred	Singapore	M.A. Th.	2000
Tinge	Ernie	Philippines	M.A. Min.	2000
Tubesa	Mila	Philippines	M.A. Th.	2000
Urbano	Donald Paul	Philippines	Grad. Cert.	2000
Akers	Matthew	USA	M.A. Miss.	2001
Angway	Donald	Philippines	M. Div.	2001
Ativo	Marita	Philippines	M. Div.	2001
Baldree	Melvin Michael	USA	M.A. Min.	2001
Bisayan	Lorenzo (Ramon)	Philippines	M.A. Miss.	2001
Budiono	Eko	Indonesia	M.A. Min.	2001
Choi	Su Nam	Korea	M.A. Th. M. Div.	2001 2003
Cole/Dalton	Deborah Kaye	USA	M. Div. D. Min.	2001 2006
Domingo	Rolando	Philippines	M.A. Min.	2001
Domingo	Oliver	Philippines	M.A. Miss. M. Div.	2001 2003
Elisa	Ide Bagus	Indonesia	M.A. Min.	2001
Girsang	Salmon	Indonesia	M.A. Min.	2001
Herawati	Lilik	Indonesia	M.A. Min.	2001

LAST NAME	FIRST NAME	HOME COUNTRY	DEGREE	YEAR GRANTED
Hong	Stephen	USA	M.A. Min. M. Div. D. Min.	2001 2005 2013
Hyun	Shin	Korea	M.A. Th.	2001
Jeong	Seong Ryeol	Korea	M.A. Miss. M. Div.	2001 2002
Kam Sheung Fai	Tony	Malaysia	M.A. Min.	2001
Kambuno	Yakolina	Indonesia	M.A. Min.	2001
Kim	Ji-Hye	Korea	M.A. Miss. M. Div.	2001 2002
Kristianto	Beni	Indonesia	M.A. Min.	2001
Lan	Loh Yim	Malaysia	M.A. Min.	2001
Libag	Jonathan Banza	Philippines	M.A. Miss.	2001
Lim	Hak Do (Joseph)	Korea	M.A. Min.	2001
Mang Pu	Peter	Myanmar	M.A. Min. M. Div.	2001 2004
Nobles	Shannon Lynn	USA	Grad. Cert. M.A. Min.	2001 2006
Pacleb	Leodegario	Philippines	M.A. Min.	2001
Park	Jin Woo	Korea	M. Div.	2001
Requina	Prospero Oberes	Philippines	M.A. Th.	2001
Rokosawa	Seru Bulai	Fiji	M.A. Th. M. Div. D. Min.	2001 2002 2015
Rumbiak	Amelia Kimberly Ann	Indonesia	M.A. Min.	2001
Ryan	Paul	USA	M.A. Mss.	2001
Scahill	Katrina	Australia	M. Div.	2001
Seko	Hiroko	Japan	Grad. Cert.	2001
Seko	Shinji	Japan	M.A. Min.	2001
Setyatmoko	Triyogo	Indonesia	M.A. Min.	2001
Shin	Hyun	Korea	M.A. Th. M. Div.	2001 2002
Soo	Jessie	Malaysia	M.A. Min.	2001
Soo	Lai Yoong "Jessie"	Malaysia	M.A. Min.	2001
Soo-Sin Lee	Sharon	Malaysia	Grad. Con. Certificate	2001
Tok Eng Beng	Benjamin	Singapore	M.A. Min.	2001

Appendix A 159

LAST NAME	FIRST NAME	HOME COUNTRY	DEGREE	YEAR GRANTED
Um	Joon Yong	Korea	M.A. Min. M. Div.	2001
Wijaya	Sunjaya	Indonesia	M.A. Min.	2001
Anoling	Alpher	Philippines	M.A. Min.	2002
Aust	Carsten	Germany	M.A. Th. M. Div. M. Th.	2002 2004 2009
Cartledge	David Frederick	Australia	M.A. Min.	2002
Cartledge	Marie Joyce	Australia	M.A. Min.	2002
Catanes	Rhea Esphyr	Philippines	Grad. Cert. M.A. Min. M. Div.	2002 2006 2008
Cruiz	Meriam	Philippines	M.A. Min.	2002
Duong	Khiem Huu	Vietnam	M.A. Min. M. Div.	2002
Gulane	Carlos	Philippines	M.A. Min.	2002
Ho	Minh Ngoc	Vietnam	M.A. Min. M. Div.	2002 2003
Ho-van den Berg	Johanna Louise	Netherlands	M.A. Intercultural Studies	2002
Kang	Young-Ju	Korea	M.A. Th. M. Div.	2002 2005
Kim	Young Hee	Korea	M.A. Intercultural Studies	2002
Kim	Kwang Han	Korea	M.A. Intercultural Studies M.A. Intercultural Studies Islamic	2002 2003
Lee	Il	Korea	M.A. Th.	2002
Lee	Sang Yun	Korea	M.A. Th. M. Div.	2002 2003
Lian	Pau Deih	Myanmar	M.A. Min.	2002
Miyake	Noriyuki	Japan	M.A. Th. M. Div. M. Th.	2002 2004 2006
Nem	Dam Sian	Myanmar	M.A. Intercultural Studies	2002
Omura	Yoshiko	Japan	M. Div.	2002
Ovsepyan	Ruben	Russia	M.A. Min. M. Div. M. Th.	2002 2003 2006

LAST NAME	FIRST NAME	HOME COUNTRY	DEGREE	YEAR GRANTED
Rice	Monte Lee	USA	M. Div.	2002
Roperos	Eduardo Jr.	Philippines	M. Div.	2002
Rupacha	Mana	Nepal	M.A. Min.	2002
Selvaratnam	Robert	Malaysia	M.A. Min.	2002
Song	Kyung Hee	Korea	M. Div.	2002
Tcherviakov	Alexander	Russia	M.A. Min. M. Div.	2002 2003
Yang	Eun Hwa	Korea	Grad. Cert.	2002
Acaso	Joel	Philippines	M.A. Th.	2003
Alay	Ricardo	Philippines	M.A. Min.	2003
Alcoran-Benavidez	Doreen	Philippines	Th. M.	2003
Chen	De Hui	China	M.A. Min.	2003
Dermawan	Agustinus	Indonesia	M. Div.	2003
Dim Lian Cing	Esther	Myanmar	M.A. Intercultural Studies M. Div.	2003 2004
Ely	Renato	Philippines	M.A. Min.	2003
Fish	Hosea	Myanmar	M.A. Intercultural Studies M. Div.	2003 2004
Garmaa	Urtnasan	Mongolia	M.A. Intercultural Studies	2003
Gutierrez	Adelina	Philippines	M.A. Min. M. Div.	2003 2004
Haaland	Jeff	USA	M. Div.	2003
Jun	Byeong Hei	Korea	M.A. Intercultural Studies Islamic	2003
Kang	Chang Soo	Korea	M.A. Intercultural Studies M. Th.	2003
Khokhar	Munnawar Naz	Pakistan	M.A. Intercultural Studies M. Div.	2003 2004
Kim	Yong Koo (Timothy)	Korea	M.A. Intercultural Studies	2003
Kim	Sang Yub	Korea	M.A. Intercultural Studies	2003
Lee	Pil Ju	Korea	M. Div.	2003
Loong	See Hwa	Malaysia	M.A. Min.	2003
Manuel	Raul	Philippines	Grad. Cert.	2003

LAST NAME	FIRST NAME	HOME COUNTRY	DEGREE	YEAR GRANTED
Mung	Lian Sian	Myanmar	M.A. Min. M. Div. M. Th.	2003 2004 2007
Nathan	Francesca Alma	Philippines	Grad. Cert.	2003
Sacdal	Luz	Philippines	M.A. Min.	2003
Santiago	Arturo	Philippines	Grad. Cert.	2003
Sunarjo	Suwanto	Indonesia	M.A. Min.	2003
Suwanto	Agustina	Indonesia	M.A. Min. M. Div.	2003 2006
Swartz	Anita	Philippines	M.A. Intercultural Studies	2003
Takatani	Mitsuyo	Japan	M.A. Th. M. Div.	2003 2004
Theis	Julia	Indonesia	M.A. Min.	2003
Vicente	Marcelo	Philippines	M.A. Min.	2003
Villanueva	Leah	Philippines	M.A. Intercultural Studies	2003
Villaroza	Elizabeth	Philippines	M.A. Min. M. Div.	2003 2005
Zhang	Qin (Edith)	China	M. Div.	2003
Bae	Peter Jin	Korea	M.A. Intercultural Studies Islamic	2004
Choi	Sung Hye	Korea	M.A. Intercultural Studies	2004
Conserman	Analyn	Philippines	M.A. Th. M. Div. D. Min.	2004 2005 2014
Das	Dennis Madhusudan	Bangladesh	M. Div.	2004
Das	Martha	Bangladesh	M. Div.	2004
Fulgencio	Ma. Nelly	Philippines	M.A. Min.	2004
Htwe	Kyaw Kyaw	Myanmar	M.A. Min. M. Div.	2004 2005
Kang	Woo Keun	Korea	M.A. Th. M. Div.	2004 2006
Langford	Richard Michael	USA	M.A. Intercultural Studies (Islamic Concentration)	2004 2005
Lim	Siew Ling	Malaysia	M.A. Min.	2004
Loke	Posuka	Indonesia	M.A. Th. M. Div.	2004

LAST NAME	FIRST NAME	HOME COUNTRY	DEGREE	YEAR GRANTED
Lole	Iosua	American Samoa	Grad. Cert. M. Div.	2005 2006
Lorenzo	Anthony	Philippines	M.A. Min.	2004
McAteer	James Michael	USA	M.A. Intercultural Studies	2004 2005
Minus	Shirley Rose	Myanmar	M. Div.	2004
Miyake	Chikako	Japan	M.A. Min.	2004
Nathan	Peter	Australia	M.A. Intercultural Studies Islamic	2004
Ordonio	Johnny	Philippines	M.A. Th.	2004
Park	Kyeong Suk	Korea	Grad. Cert.	2004
Phattanavioj	Suphat	Thailand	M.A Min. M. Div.	2004 2005
Piang	Zam Sian	Myanmar	M.A. Th. M. Div.	2004 2005
Pulepule	Faatuatua	Samoa	M.A. Min. M. Div	2004 2012
Sardjono	Djoni	Indonesia	M.A. Intercultural Studies Islamic	2004
Yan	Mian Hua	China	M.A. Min. M. Div.	2004 2005
Yoon	Chang Jae (Moses)	Korea	M.A. Intercultural Studies	2004
Abasolo	Zenaida	Philippines	M.A. Intercultural Studies	2005
Acena	Helen	Philippines	M.A. Min. M. Div.	2005 2009
Balanguiwed	Evangeline	Philippines	M.A. Intercultural Studies Islamic	2005
Banggo	Danilo	Philippines	M.A. Min.	2005
Batiyaka	Selina	Samoa	M.A. Min.	2005
Carable	Marife	Philippines	M. Th.	2005
Cheum	Chee Wai (David)	Singapore	M.A. Min.	2005
Cork	Ngatupuna	Fiji	M.A. Min.	2005
Covert	Dennis	Fiji	M. Div.	2005
Covert	Melanie	USA	M.A. Min.	2005

LAST NAME	FIRST NAME	HOME COUNTRY	DEGREE	YEAR GRANTED
Dawson	Connie	USA	M.A. Th. M. Div.	2005 2006
Dorimon	Rey	Philippines	M.A. Min. M. Div.	2005 2007
Godwin	Robert	USA	M.A. Min.	2005
Hamm	Charles James	Canada	M.A. Min.	2005
Kao	Sheng Fu	Taiwan	M.A. Th. M. Div.	2005 2006
Kitajima	Ayako	Japan	M.A. Intercultural Studies	2005
Kuruwale	Vilive Toka	Fiji	M.A. Min.	2005
Lee	In Jae	Korea	M.A. Min.	2005
Lim	Ma. Teresita	Philippines	M.A. Min.	2005
Ngwar	Zar Char	Myanmar	M.A. Min. M. Div.	2005 2017
Nwosu	Theresia Ateh	Cameroon	Grad. Cert.	2005
Ong	Seng Chai Bernard	Malaysia	M.A. Min.	2005
Peter	Andrew Mohanraj	Malaysia	M.A. Min.	2005
Piang	Thian Nun	Myanmar	M. Div.	2005
Rizado	Regalado	Philippines	M.A. Th. M. Div.	2005
Ross	Denise	Ireland	M.A. Th. M. Div.	2005
Schowalter	Thomas	Germany	M.A. Intercultural Studies Islamic	2005
Shaloa (Lou Ming Hui)		China	M. Div.	2005
Thang	Luan Khen Khaw	Myanmar	M.A. Min. M. Div. Ph. D.	2005 2007 2023
Tora	Laisiasa	Fiji	M.A. Min.	2005
Tupamahu	Ekaputra	Indonesia	M.A. Th. M. Div.	2005
Vacayatu	Tawatatau	Fiji	M.A. Min.	2005
Woo	Won Sik	Korea	M.A. Intercultural Studies	2005
Yoshihara	Hirokatsu	Japan	M.A. Th. M. Div.	2005

LAST NAME	FIRST NAME	HOME COUNTRY	DEGREE	YEAR GRANTED
Acena	Michael	Philippines	M. Div.	2006
Alvarez	Benjamin Lyndon	Philippines	M.A. Min.	2006
Asuncion	Rodel	Philippines	M.A. Min.	2006
Bainivalu	Jope	Fiji	M.A. Min.	2006
Batibasaga	Apenisa Vitau	Fiji	M.A. Min.	2006
Caigoy	Rebecca	Philippines	Grad. Cert. M.A. Min.	2006 2022
Chin	Phong Tuck Peter	Malaysia	M.A. Min.	2006
Chin	Bee Wan Evonne	Malaysia	M.A. Min.	2006
Choi	Young Ja	Korea	M.A. Th. M. Div.	2006
Cing	Dim Lun	Myanmar	M.A. Min.	2006
Dela Cruz	Rowell	Philippines	M.A. Min.	2006
Dunn	Ralph Peter Meissner	Fiji	M.A. Min.	2006
Fatialofa	Frederick Tautala	New Zealand	M.A. Min. M. Div.	2006 2015
Gadingan	Saturnino	Philippines	M.A. Min. M. Div	2006 2012
Gan	Kee Hock Jeremiah	Malaysia	M.A. Min.	2006
Han	Kyung Ja	Japan	M.A. Intercultural Studies	2006
Ho	Geok Choom Danny	Singapore	M.A. Min.	2006
Kereti	Levi Jr.	New Zealand	M.A. Th.	2006
Lim	Kia Ching Kelvin	Singapore	M.A. Min.	2006
Lin	Zarni Kyaw	Myanmar	M.A. Min.	2006
Mung	Kham Hau	Myanmar	M. Div.	2006
Myint	Khin soe	Myanmar	M.A. Min.	2006
Nam	Ha Hyun	Korea	M.A. Th. M. Div.	2006
Naulago	Illisoni	Fiji	M.A. Min.	2006
Ngoh	Moon Tee	Malaysia	M.A. Min.	2006
Ogino	Michio	Japan	M.A. Th. M. Div.	2006 2008
Oh	Syeung-Myung	Korea	M.A. Th.	2006
Penserga	Elizabeth	Philippines	M.A. Min.	2006
Pipkin	Brian Keith	USA	M.A. Intercultural Studies	2006
Pipkin	Shannon Marie	USA	M.A. Intercultural Studies	2006

LAST NAME	FIRST NAME	HOME COUNTRY	DEGREE	YEAR GRANTED
Sae Tae	Sujirat	Thailand	M.Div	2006
Sherman	Jayesun Israel	USA	M.A. Th.	2006
Sivoinavatu	Mesake Loke	Fiji	M.A. Th. M. Div. D. Min.	2006 2019
Sohn	You Kil	Korea	M.A. Th.	2006
Stefan	Robert	USA	M. Div.	2006
Sun	Dezhi	China	M. Div.	2006
Swe	Nini	Myanmar	M.A. Min.	2006
Tan	Jiali	China	M. Div.	2006
Tan	Yew Fook	Malaysia	M.A. Min.	2006
Thang	Tuan Suan	Myanmar	M.A. Min.	2006
Trotter	John	USA	M.A. Intercultural Studies	2006
Tun	Aung Moe	Myanmar	M.A. Min. M. Div.	2006 2009
Ugboh	Godspower Peter	Nigeria	M.A. Intercultural Studies	2006
Ware	Anthony James	Australia	M.A. Min.	2006
Yong Heng Khoon	Gideon	Malaysia	M.A. Min.	2006
Za Thang	Pau Thawn	Myanmar	M.A. Min.	2006
Aipolo	Ane Sesimoni Soraya	Tonga	Grad. Cert. M.A. Min.	2007 2022
Anderson	Lew	USA	M.A. Intercultural Studies	2007
Aquino	Abelardo	Philippines	M.A. Min.	2007
Baldonado	Teddy	Philippines	M.A. Min. M. Div.	2007 2017
Basco	Marjorie	Philippines	M.A. Min.	2007
Belgarde	Jonathan	USA	M. Div.	2007
Belino/Cruz	Mehden	Philippines	M.A. Intercultural Studies	2007
Bercero	Joseph Neil	Philippines	M.A. Th.	2007
Dawson	Bruce	USA	M.A. Intercultural Studies	2007
Forsberg	Steven	USA	M.A. Min.	2007
Galacan	Esther	Philippines	M.A. Intercultural Studies	2007

LAST NAME	FIRST NAME	HOME COUNTRY	DEGREE	YEAR GRANTED
Inio	Morcita	Philippines	M. Div.	2007
Kim	Byeong Kuk	Korea	M. Div.	2007
Mataia	Sila	New Zealand	M.A. Th.	2007
Moe	Aung Kyaw	Myanmar	M.A. Min.	2007
Pasion	Arnulfo	Philippines	M. Div.	2007
Seb	Rushulo	India	M.A. Intercultural Studies	2007
Uminga	Alejandro	Philippines	M.A. Min.	2007
Yoo	Hun (Jabez)	Korea	M. Div.	2007
Zunduidorj	Bayaraa	Mongolia	M.A. Th.	2007
Beard	David	USA	M.A. Min.	2008
Bustria	Dominador	Philippines	M.A. Min. / M. Div.	2008 / 2012
Dela Cruz	Saul	Philippines	M.A. Intercultural Studies	2008
Durene	Mark Arthur	USA	M.A. Intercultural Studies	2008
Hughes	Angela	New Zealand	M.A. Intercultural Studies	2008
Jones	Carrie Renee	USA	M.A. Intercultural Studies	2008
Jun	Jung Hwan	Korea	M. Div.	2008
Kim	Yoon Uoo	Korea	D. Min.	2008
Kim	Jun	Korea	M.A. Th. / M. Div.	2008 / 2009
Koh	Chew Heong	Malaysia	M.A. Intercultural Studies	2008
Niebres-Hortizuela	Marlene Agnes	Philippines	M.A. Intercultural Studies	2008
Pandey	Amar	Nepal	M. Div.	2008
Roslim	Ora Isabella	Indonesia	M.A. Min.	2008
Roslim	Daniel Stephanus	Indonesia	M.A. Th. / M. Div.	2008 / 2010
Salcedo	Edgar	Philippines	M.A. Th.	2008
Sanglay	Hilario	Philippines	Grad. Cert.	2008
Seala	Mataia Jr.	Samoa	M.A. Min.	2008
Snider	William	USA	M.A. Intercultural Studies	2008
Tran-qui	Duc Laurent	France	M. Div.	2008

Appendix A 167

LAST NAME	FIRST NAME	HOME COUNTRY	DEGREE	YEAR GRANTED
Angeles	Jay	Philippines	M.A. Intercultural Studies	2009
Aquino	Imelda	Philippines	M. Div.	2009
Bañares	Jose Jorge	Philippines	M.A. Th.	2009
Batiyaka	Vereniki	Fiji	M.A. Th.	2009
Chun	Jae Youn	Korea	M.A. Intercultural Studies M. Div.	2009 2010
Cuvatoka	Eroni	Fiji	M.A. Min.	2009
Fernando	Reynaldo	Philippines	M.A. Min.	2009
Haber	Aurelio	Philippines	M.A. Min.	2009
Hicks	A. Flint	Fiji	M.A. Th.	2009
Hicks	Kazel	Fiji	M.A. Min.	2009
Kang	Im Seok (David)	Korea	M. Div.	2009
Kim	Woong Tae	Korea	M.A. Th.	2009
Kwarteng	Lawrence	Ghana	Grad. Cert.	2009
Lim	Zaldy	Philippines	Grad. Cert. M.A. Min.	2009 2013
Mataika	Josaia	Fiji	M.A. Th.	2009
Monares	Junray	Philippines	M.A. Intercultural Studies	2009
Rauca	Mosese	Fiji	M.A. Min.	2009
Richardson	Deanna Yvonne	USA	M.A. Min. M. Div.	2009 2016
Tran-qui	An Thien (Lydia)	Vietnam	M. Div.	2009
Amma	Masamichi	Japan	M.A. Min.	2010
Amma	Tokiko	Japan	Grad. Cert.	2010
Baniwas	Benjamin	Philippines	M.A. Min. M. Div.	2010 2013
Batsuren	Enkhbayar	Mongolia	M.A. Min.	2010
Clements	Darin	USA	M.A. Min. M. Div. Ph.D	2010 2014 2019
Cruz	Glenn Sanvictores	Philippines	M.A. Intercultural Studies	2010
Dionisio	Judy	Philippines	M.A. Th.	2010
Dutcher	Roger	USA	M. Div.	2010
Echavez	Nixon	Philippines	M.A. Intercultural Studies	2010

LAST NAME	FIRST NAME	HOME COUNTRY	DEGREE	YEAR GRANTED
Fatialofa	Martha	New Zealand	M.A. Min. / M. Div.	2010 / 2016
Hariono	Poedji	Indonesia	Grad. Cert.	2010
Hiramatsu	Gen	Japan	M. Div.	2010
Hortizuela	Ryan	Philippines	M. Div.	2010
Kim	Daljin	Korea	M.A. Min.	2010
Kim	Jeong Doo	Korea	M.A. Intercultural Studies	2010
Koh	Kok Tiong Ben	Singapore	M. Div.	2010
Kopa	Lafaele	New Zealand	M.A. Min.	2010
Mina	Wilfred	Philippines	M.A. Min.	2010
Oh	In-Kyoung	Korea	M.A. Intercultural Studies Islamic	2010
Park	Youn Jung (Cara)	Korea	M.A. Th. / M. Div.	2010 / 2014
Parrish	Evelyn Paige	USA	Grad. Cert. / M.A. Min.	2010 / 2016
Pugong	Benjamin	Philippines	M.A. Th.	2010
Pyoun	Jung Suk (Joy)	Korea	M.A. Min.	2010
Su	Yan Zong (Selena)	China	M.A. Min.	2010
Toilolo	Leatuolo-Mabel	Samoa	M. Div.	2010
Vesiloto	Vasemaca	Fiji	M. Div.	2010
Wijaya	Linda	Indonesia	Grad. Con. Certificate	2010
Yong	Chin Sii (Daniel)	Malaysia	M.A. Min.	2010
Yoo	Kyung Jun (Rey)	Korea	M.A. Min. / M. Div	2010 / 2012
Zineemeder	Munkhjargal	Mongolia	Grad. Cert.	2010
Qin	Da (Daniel)	China	M. Div / M.Th.	2011 / 2016
Alingbas	Precila	Philippines	M.A. Intercultural Studies	2011
Aquino	Arlano	Philippines	M.A. Th.	2011
Aumua	Suliveta	Samoa	M.A. Min.	2011
Bowdoin	Shellie	USA	M.A. Min.	2011
Dillemuth	William	USA	M.A. Intercultural Studies	2011
German	Stuart	USA	M.A. Min.	2011

LAST NAME	FIRST NAME	HOME COUNTRY	DEGREE	YEAR GRANTED
Maeng	Mi Young	Korea	M.A. Intercultural Studies	2011
Moananu	Taeleipu	New Zealand	M.A. Min. M. Div.	2011 2014
Nakagawa	Yuri	Japan	M.A. Intercultural Studies M. Div.	2011 2013
Obeng	Joshua	Ghana	M.A. Th.	2011
Ong	Thiam Boon (Bernard)	Malaysia	M.A. Intercultural Studies	2011
Phanon	Panthakan	Thailand	M.Div	2011
Phanon	Suree	Thailand	M.A. Min.	2011
Shwe	Stephen Sein	Myanmar	M.A. Min. M. Div. M. Th.	2011 2014 2023
Tamale-Oh	Hensel	Philippines	M. Div.	2011
Tejedo	Carolyn	Philippines	M.A. Min.	2011
Torres	April Rosse Majan	Philippines	M.A. Min.	2011
Torres	William Bill	Philippines	M. Div.	2011
Wang	Min (Gloria)	China	M.A. Intercultural Studies	2011
Yang	Changyong (Joel)	Korea	M. Div.	2011
Bilog	Allan	Philippines	M. Div.	2012
Chen	Chiu-Yun (Joy)	Taiwan	M.A. Intercultural Studies	2012
Cho	Min Hwan (Isaac)	Korea	M.A. Min. M. Div.	2012 2014
Choi	Moon Hyun	Korea	M.A. Th. M. Div.	2012 2014
Chung	Youjin (Daniel)	Korea	M. Div.	2012
Du	Yan (Menorah)	China	M.A. Theo.	2012
Hiramatsu	Kei	Japan	M.A. Min.	2012
Hsu	Yu-Ching (Renae)	Taiwan	M. Div.	2012
Kim	Joo Young (Caleb)	Korea	M. Div.	2012
Lee	Christine	Australia	M.A. Intercultural Studies	2012
Lee	Dong Hyung (Paul)	Korea	M.A. Min.	2012
Lee	Tae Hyun (DJ)	Korea	M. Div.	2012
Lester	Craig	USA	Grad. Cert.	2012
Masarate	Ricky	Philippines	M. Div.	2012

LAST NAME	FIRST NAME	HOME COUNTRY	DEGREE	YEAR GRANTED
McNelis	Helen	Philippines	M.A. Min	2012
Parrish	Kent Ryan	USA	M. Div.	2012
Paul	Rebecca	Pakistan	M.A. Min.	2012
Peña	Michael	Philippines	M.A. Min.	2012
Samau	Napalu Sam	Australia	M.A. Intercultural Studies Islamic	2012
Smith	Sophin	Cambodia	M.A. Min.	2012
Tahitoe	Mario	Indonesia	M. Div.	2012
Taypoc	Manolo	Philippines	M.A. Min.	2012
Tesoro	Chester Allan	Philippines	M. Div.	2012
Turney	Russell	USA	D. Min.	2012
Vretonko	Roman	Czech Republic	M.A. Min.	2012
Vretonko	Rut	Czech Republic	M.A. Intercultural Studies	2012
Williams	Jason Scott	USA	M.A. Intercultural Studies M. Div.	2012 2013
Arquero	Brian Bailey	Philippines	M. Div.	2013
Arukua	Donna	Papua New Guinea	M. Div.	2013
Bull	George	Fiji	M.A. Min.	2013
Chen	Pei-Chiao (Scottie)	Taiwan	M. Div.	2013
Cheung	Wai Leung (Leon)	Hong Kong	M. Div.	2013
Dionson	Herman	Philippines	M. Div.	2013
Hoertig	Stephan	Switzerland	Grad. Cert.	2013
Huang	Qun Huan (Kelly)	China	M.A. Intercultural Studies M. Div.	2013 2016
Hung	Shih-Yin (Melody)	Taiwan	M. Div.	2013
Jung	Hyun Gyun (Steven)	Korea	M.A. Min. M. Div.	2013 2015
Kim	Jin Kwang (Lucien)	Korea	M. Div.	2013
Lee	Junghee (Dave)	Korea	M. Div.	2013
Lee	Misoon (Michelle)	Korea	M. Div.	2013
Ma	No Mi (Naomi)	Myanmar	M. Div.	2013
Matakaca	Apisai	Fiji	M. Div.	2013
McNelis	Francis	USA	M. Div.	2013
Pinzon	Michael James	Philippines	M. Div.	2013

Appendix A 171

LAST NAME	FIRST NAME	HOME COUNTRY	DEGREE	YEAR GRANTED
Rosal	Russell Rolf	Philippines	M.A. Intercultural Studies	2013
Sha	Yu (Mandy)	China	M. Div.	2013
Shen	Chunxiu (Grace)	China	M.A. Intercultural Studies	2013
Steen	Robin	USA	M.A. Intercultural Studies	2013
Steen	Susan	USA	M.A. Intercultural Studies	2013
Toilolo	Tinou Bill	Samoa	M.A. Min. M. Div.	2013 2016
Tuang	Nang Khan (Moses)	Myanmar	M. Div.	2013
Veitaladrua	Savenaca	Fiji	M.A. Min.	2013
Victa	Carlo Nazareno	USA	Grad. Cert. M. Div.	2013 2015
Vueta	Naomi	Fiji	M.A. Min.	2013
Warren	Christopher	Samoa	M.A. Min.	2013
Annoque	Marcelina	Philippines	M.A. Min.	2014
Avealalo	Alapati	Samoa	M.A. Min. M. Div.	2014 2015
Balite	Joshua	Philippines	M.A. Intercultural Studies	2014
Conceja	Solimar	Philippines	M.A. Th. M. Div.	2014 2017
Jung	Phil Joo (Jesse)	Korea	M. Div.	2014
Kang	Young-Sam (Jeremy)	Korea	M.A. Min. M. Div.	2014 2015
Khai	Kham Sian	Myanmar	Grad. Cert. M.A. Min. M. Div.	2014 2015 2016
Lalrongheta	Robert Lal	Myanmar	M. Div.	2014
Lee	Sherry	USA	M.A. Intercultural Studies M. Div.	2014 2016
Len	Sui Khaw	Myanmar	M. Div.	2014
Liu	Man (Amanda)	China	M. Div.	2014
Pell	Elizabeth Ashley	USA	M.A. Inter. Studies M. Div.	2014 2021
Rajapakse	Ann Mitchelle	Sri Lanka	M.A. Min.	2014
Seniloli	Taniela	Fiji	M.A. Min.	2014
Tucker	Kevin	USA	M. Div.	2014

LAST NAME	FIRST NAME	HOME COUNTRY	DEGREE	YEAR GRANTED
Yao	Stephen	China	M. Div.	2014
Zhang	Li	China	Grad. Cert. M.A. Th. M. Div.	2014 2015 2020
Callena	Lucena	Philippines	M. Div.	2015
Chin Lai	Khinsar (Davidson)	Myanmar	M.A. Intercultural Studies M. Div.	2015 2017
De Borja	Annabelle	Philippines	M.A. Intercultural Studies	2015
Dong	Meng (Deborah)	China	M.A. Min. (Chinese Program)	2015
Echasa	Dedani Mwemedi	Republic of Congo	M.A. Intercultural Studies	2015
Huang	Kaixin (David)	China	B.A. Min. (Chinese Program) M.A. Min. (Chinese Program)	2015 2016
Lausa	Ferlyn Joy	Philippines	Grad. Cert. M.A. Intercultural Studies	2015 2016
Liu	Lijuan (Ruth)	China	B.A. Min. (Chinese Program) M.A. Min. (Chinese Program)	2015 2016
Ly	Dareth Anthony	USA	M.A. Min.	2015
McClure	Benjamin	USA	M.A. Min.	2015
Millares	Jaylord	Philippines	M. Div.	2015
Ocbina	Lanilane	Philippines	M.A. Intercultural Studies	2015
Otculan	Gilmore	Philippines	M. Div.	2015
Prakash	Dhan	India	M. Th.	2015
Puckett	Jeffrey	USA	Grad. Cert. M. Div.	2015 2016
Pulami	Saraswati Thapa	Nepal	M.A. Min.	2015
Ratna	Adlina	Bangladesh	Grad. Cert. M.A. Intercultural Studies	2015 2016
Robinette	Frank Kelly	USA	M.A. Min.	2015

Appendix A 173

LAST NAME	FIRST NAME	HOME COUNTRY	DEGREE	YEAR GRANTED
Samblero	Narlo	Philippines	M.A. Min.	2015
Sicam	Jherssey Belle	Philippines	Grad. Cert.	2015
Singh	Sunil	Nepal	M. Div.	2015
Wang	Hang (Bettina)	China	M. Div.	2015
Zam	Pau Suan	Myanmar	Grad. Cert. M. Div.	2015 2015
Aumua	Seugalupe	Samoa	M.A. Min.	2016
Cai	Zhen Qing (Nissi)	China	M. Div.	2016
Candole	Nancy	Philippines	M.A. Min.	2016
Co	Joey Albert	Philippines	M.A. Min.	2016
Dana	Edwin	Philippines	M.A. Min.	2016
Devi (Kopana)	Estika	Fiji	M.A. Min.	2016
Fata	Faafetai	Samoa	M.A. Min.	2016
Fuimaono	Della	American Samoa	M.A. Min.	2016
G	Chang Bawng (Simon)	Myanmar	M. Div.	2016
Gurning	John Yeremia	Indonesia	M. Div.	2016
Kam	Sung Woo (Yohan)	Korea	M.A. Th. M. Div.	2016 2017
Kao	Kuei-Hui (Amy)	Taiwan	M.A. Min. (Chinese Program)	2016 2018
Kim	Jeong Sik (Joshua)	Korea	M.A. Min.	2016
Labenio	Ayan Clifford	Philippines	M.A. Th. M. Div.	2016 2017
Li	Ye Li (Lili)	Myanmar	M.A. Min. M. Div.	2016 2018
Liu	Hua Tun (Daniel)	China	M. Div.	2016
Mikaele	Paulo	Samoa	M.A. Min.	2016
Mose	Lotaua	Samoa	M.A. Min.	2016
Park	Youngsoo (Jerome)	Korea	M. Div.	2016
Perudurayalage	Shamgar Emmanuwel	Sri Lanka	Grad. Cert. M.A. Min. M. Div.	2016 2017 2020
Qioniwasa	Isoa	Fiji	M.A. Min. M. Div.	2016
Ratna	Mrinal (Mark)	Bangladesh	M. Div.	2016
Remikatu	Jefri Hina	Indonesia	M.A. Th.	2016
Stowers	Afa	Samoa	M.A. Min.	2016

LAST NAME	FIRST NAME	HOME COUNTRY	DEGREE	YEAR GRANTED
Su	Mon (Grace)	Myanmar	M. Div.	2016
Subang	Jemon	Philippines	M.A. Th. M. Div.	2016 2017
Tao	Jichun (Luke)	China	B.A. Min. (Chinese Program) M.A. Min. (Chinese Program)	2016 2017
Tictica	Baltazar	Philippines	M.A. Min.	2016
Tofilau	Sinapati	Samoa	M.A. Min.	2016
Toilolo	Penerosa	Samoa	M.A. Min.	2016
Tora	Jasa	Fiji	M.A. Min.	2016
Tuigamala	Vaalele	American Samoa	M.A. Min.	2016
Victa	Patricia	Philippines	Grad. Cert.	2016
Vulakouvaki	Epineri	Fiji	M.A. Th. M. Div.	2016 2018
Wu	Qiongfang (Grace)	China	M.A. Intercultural Studies M. Div.	2016 2017
Zhang	Yuan Ye (Elma)	China	M. Div.	2016
Zin	Kyi Kyi	Myanmar	M.A. Min. M. Div.	2016 2017
An	Jung Ja (Sue)	Korea	M.A. Th.	2017
Aung	Phi (Shepherd)	Myanmar	M. Div.	2017
Ch'ng	Gan Wee (Rachel)	Malaysia	M.A. Intercultural Studies	2017
Cornelio Arias	Misael	Dominican Republic	M.A. Intercultural Studies	2017
Ding	Qun	China	B.A. Min. (Chinese Program) M.A. Min. (Chinese Program)	2017 2018
Du	Zaw Seng (Gabriel)	Myanmar	M. Div.	2017
Faumuina	Alofa	Samoa	M.A. Min.	2017
Flores	Rhodeliza Joyce	Philippines	M. Div.	2017
Gabuay	Billy	Philippines	M. Div.	2017

Appendix A 175

LAST NAME	FIRST NAME	HOME COUNTRY	DEGREE	YEAR GRANTED
Ge	Xinxin (Christina)	China	B.A. Min. (Chinese Program)	2017
Hu	Congzhen (Lily)	China	B.A. Min. (Chinese Program)	2017
Iosefa	Tili Teo Magele	New Zealand	M.A. Min. M. Div.	2017 2018
Jeon	Myong Soo (Luke)	Korea	M.A. Intercultural Studies	2017
Khai	Thang Khan	Myanmar	M. Div.	2017
Kopana	Trevor	Solomon Islands	M. Div.	2017
Kumi	Francis	Ghana	M. Div.	2017
Kyaw	Min Naing (Joseph)	Myanmar	Grad. Cert.	2017
Li	Dalin	China	B.A. Min. (Chinese Program)	2017
Li	Enhui (Grace)	China	M.A. Min. (Chinese Program)	2017
Li	Jie (Sophia)	China	B.A. Min. (Chinese Program) M.A. Intercultural Studies	2017 2019
Limwas	Joan	Philippines	M.A. Min. M. Div.	2017 2019
Lovelace	Joshua	USA	M.A. Intercultural Studies	2017
Mangosan	Angelita	Philippines	M.A. Min.	2017
Mao	Yuan	China	B.A. Min. (Chinese Program) M.A. Min. (Chinese Program)	2017 2018
Nari	Josiah	Papua New Guinea	M.A. Min.	2017
Oh	Oun Mi (Sarah)	Korea	M.A. Intercultural Studies	2017
Oracion-Dagami	Glory Mae	Philippines	M.A. Min.	2017
Oseso	Dorothy Elavaya	Kenya	M.A. Th. M. Div.	2017 2020

LAST NAME	FIRST NAME	HOME COUNTRY	DEGREE	YEAR GRANTED
Pulepule	Abraham Ueiti	Australia	M.A. Min. M. Div.	2017 2018
Tao	Yufa	China	B.A. Min. (Chinese Program) M.A. Min. (Chinese Program)	2017 2018
Uchimura	Aya	Japan	M. Div.	2017
Velasco	Buenavielyn	Philippines	Grad. Cert. M.A. Intercultural Studies	2017 2018
Wang	Min (Emma)	China	M.A. Min. (Chinese Program)	2017
Wu	Ruilong	China	B.A. Min. (Chinese Program) M.A. Min. (Chinese Program)	2017 2018
Almonte Peña	Debora	Dominican Republic	M.A. Intercultural Education	2018
Bryner	Khuyen	Vietnam	M.A. Min.	2018
Cha	Yun Hee (Ruth)	Korea	M. Div.	2018
Chan	Sarah	Myanmar	M. Div.	2018
Cortez III	Claudio	Philippines	Grad. Cert. M.A. Min.	2018 2018
Fa'asala	Arlene	American Samoa	M.A. Min. M. Div.	2018 2019
Ganbold	Ninjin	Mongolia	M.A. Th.	2018
Getgaew	Chatchanin (Prince)	Thailand	M. Div.	2018
He	Yan Ni	China	B.A. Min. (Chinese Program) MA. Min (Chinese program)	2018 2019
Huang	Li li	China	B.A. Min. (Chinese Program) M.A. Min. (Chinese Program)	2018 2019

LAST NAME	FIRST NAME	HOME COUNTRY	DEGREE	YEAR GRANTED
Jia	Junfeng	China	B.A. Min. (Chinese Program)	2018
Jin	Young Hun (Paul)	Korea	M.A. Intercultural Studies	2018
Kao	Mo-Hsi (Moses)	Taiwan	M. Div.	2018
Kham	Timothy Dawt	Myanmar	M. Div.	2018
Khup	Suan Khan	Myanmar	M. Div.	2018
Lee	Sukjin (Paul)	Korea	M. Div.	2018
Li	Yong	China	B.A. Min. (Chinese Program) M.A. Min. (Chinese Program)	2018 2019
Meng	Ying	China	M.A. Min. (Chinese Program)	2018
Mo	Fan-Chi (Andrew)	Taiwan	M.A. Min.	2018
Nguyen	Huyen Thi Thanh (Bee)	Vietnam	M. Div.	2018
Pa Rongre	Vallenryan Arthur	Indonesia	M.A. Min.	2018
Pattaramong-konket	Hattakit (James)	Thailand	Grad. Cert.	2018
Pious	Ambrose	Pakistan	M.A. Th. M. Div.	2018 2019
Sharma	Sushil	Nepal	M.A. Th. M. Div.	2018 2019
Song	Wenyi	China	B.A. Min. (Chinese Program)	2018
Subong	Christopher	Philippines	Grad. Cert.	2018
Sun	Kechao (Mark)	China	B.A. Min. (Chinese Program) M.A. Min. (Chinese Program)	2018 2019
Thang	Khup Pian	Myanmar	M. Div.	2018
Tupou	Mefiposeta	Samoa	M.A. Min.	2018
Weiss	Emanuel	Switzerland	M.A. Th.	2018
Wu	Yue Rong (Helen)	China	M.A. Intercultural Education	2018

LAST NAME	FIRST NAME	HOME COUNTRY	DEGREE	YEAR GRANTED
Xiang	Xuelun (Amber)	China	B.A. Min. (Chinese Program)	2018
Yamasaki	Ginjiro	Japan	M.A. Intercultural Studies	2018
Yoo	Young Hoon (Stanley)	Korea	M.A. Intercultural Studies	2018
Zhou	Zongyue (Henry)	China	M.A. Min. (Chinese Program)	2018
Amosa	Tauinaola	Samoa	M.A. Min.	2019
Angeles	Eric K.	USA	M.A. Min.	2019
Badamjav	Davaasuren	Mongolia	M.A. Min.	2019
Caballero	Sarah Joy	Philippines	M.A. Th. / M. Div.	2019 / 2020
Calion	Agustino	Philippines	M.A. Min.	2019
Chen	Chi-neng	Taiwan	M.A. Min.	2019
Hansen	Justin	Thailand	M.A. Intercultural Studies	2019
Hari	Benjamin	Papua New Guinea	M.A. Min.	2019
Hilario	Micah Anne	Philippines	M.A. Min.	2019
Hpi	Sang Doung	Myanmar	M.A. Min.	2019
Jameson	Sharon Elizabeth	USA	Grad. Cert. / M.A. Th.	2019
Kim	Eungdap	Korea	M. Div.	2019
Li	Guang Ming	China	B.A. Min. (Chinese Program) / M.A. Min. (Chinese Program)	2019 / 2020
Liu	Min	China	B.A. Min. (Chinese Program)	2019
Long	Qing Lan	China	B.A. Min. (Chinese Program)	2019
Lopez	Jeremiah James	Philippines	M. Div.	2019
Mendoza	Llana Mae	Philippines	Grad. Cert. / M.A. Min.	2019 / 2019
Nar	Rose	Myanmar	M. Div.	2019

LAST NAME	FIRST NAME	HOME COUNTRY	DEGREE	YEAR GRANTED
Nwe	San	Myanmar	M. Div.	2019
Peng	Amin (Amphore)	China	B.A. Min. (Chinese Program)	2019
Rana	Madhuri	Nepal	M. Div.	2019
Ravenhill	Lisa	USA	M.A. Intercultural Education	2019
Santonia	Jireh	Philippines	M. Div.	2019
Sefo	Lopa	New Zealand	M.A. Min.	2019
Shwe	Hannah	Myanmar	M. Div.	2019
Song	Ancheol	Korea	M.A. Min.	2019
Toh Wee Lin	William	Singapore	D. Min.	2019
Wangmo	Namgay	Bhutan	M. Div.	2019
Xie	Bingru	China	M. Div.	2019
Xiong	Chunmei (Angelia)	China	B.A. Min. (Chinese Program) M.A. Min. (Chinese Program)	2019 2021
Zhang	Ya Huang	China	B.A. Min. (Chinese Program) M.A. Min. (Chinese Program)	2019
Zhang	Su Rong	China	B.A. Min. (Chinese Program) M.A. Min. (Chinese Program)	2019 2020
Angeles	Eunice	USA	M.A. Intercultural Studies	2020
Aung	Tun Yadanar	Myanmar	M. Div.	2020
Bavon	Rusco Stephen	Fiji	M.A. Min.	2020
Cheng	Juan Juan	China	B.A. Min. (Chinese Program) M.A. Min. (Chinese Program)	2020 2020

LAST NAME	FIRST NAME	HOME COUNTRY	DEGREE	YEAR GRANTED
Kwak	Wook Jin	Korea	M. Div.	2020
Li	Mao Yao	China	B.A. Min. (Chinese Program)	2020
Lilomaiava	Saumani	Samoa	M.A. Min.	2020
Luo	Yan	China	B.A. Min. (Chinese Program) M.A. Min. (Chinese Program)	2020 2022
Manoharan Dhanapaul	Jim Regan Paul	India	M.A. Min. M. Div.	2020 2023
Mendoza Rodriguez	Claudia Janneth	Colombia	M.A. Intercultural Studies (Islamic Concentration)	2020
Molato	Joemarie	Philippines	M.A. Min.	2020
Morisa	Daniel	USA	M.A. Min. M. Div.	2020 2022
Olayvar	Joel	Philippines	M. Div.	2020
Ortiz Quiroz	Jessica Viviana	Colombia	M.A. Intercultural Studies	2020
Ponce	Harley	Philippines	M. Div.	2020
Ren	Tiang Tiang	China	M. Div.	2020
Rodriguez	Aires Mia Amor	Philippines	M.A. Min.	2020
Salazar Carrasco	Jefte	Spain	M.A. International Studies (Islamic Concentration) M. Div.	2020 2022
Timenia	Lora	Philippines	M. Th.	2020
Wang	Yong	China	M. Div.	2020
Wang	Yunchao	China	B.A. Min. (Chinese Program)	2020
Wang	Qi (Christina)	China	B.A. Min. (Chinese Program) M.A. Min. (Chinese Program)	2020 2021
Xu	Gan Lai	China	M. Div.	2020

Appendix A

LAST NAME	FIRST NAME	HOME COUNTRY	DEGREE	YEAR GRANTED
Yang	Bide	China	B.A. Min. (Chinese Program)	2020
Yoo	Mi Seon	Korea	Grad. Cert.	2020
Zhang	Chao	China	B.A. Min. (Chinese Program)	2020
Bi	Guangmei (Amy)	China	M.A. Min. (Chinese Program)	2021
Calpi	Darlyn	Philippines	M. Div.	2021
Chawan	Kailash	Bhutan	M.A. Min.	2021
Chen	Xiaomin (Peace)	China	M.A. Min.	2021
Faumuina	Faamanuivavega	Australia	M.A. Min.	2021
Gaima	Samson James	Papua New Guinea	M.A. Min.	2021
Hashmat	Joshua	Pakistan	M. Div.	2021
He	Zhuli (Julie)	China	M.A. Min. (Chinese Program)	2021
Huang	Kailin (Timothy)	China	M.A. Min. (Chinese Program)	2021
Kap	Lian Khai	Myanmar	M.A. Th.	2021
Kyaw	Sha Khaw Ram	Myanmar	D. Min.	2021
Leaupepetele	Tusi Junior	New Zealand	M. Div.	2021
Lemalu Soi Nofoaiga	Sinapi	Samoa	M.A. Min.	2021
Liu	Ning (Zenia)	China	M. Div.	2021
Liu	Gong-Yi (Nathan)	Taiwan	B.A. Min. (Chinese Program) M.A. Min. (Chinese Program)	2021 2022
Mahara	Kiran	Nepal	M. Div.	2021
Mascay	Laurence	Philippines	D. Min.	2021
Mayyam	David Ray	Philippines	M.A. Min.	2021
Miller	Raymond	USA	D. Min.	2021
Palpeg	Neferty	Philippines	Grad. Cert. M.A. Min.	2021 2022
Pinzon	Samuel	Philippines	D. Min.	2021

LAST NAME	FIRST NAME	HOME COUNTRY	DEGREE	YEAR GRANTED
Qiu	Wenyu (Walter)	China	M. Div.	2021
Timenia	Karlo	Philippines	M. Div.	2021
Usu	Peter Pose	New Zealand	M.A. Th. M. Div.	2021
Xie	Meiqin (Sarah)	China	M.A. Min. (Chinese Program)	2021
Ye	Li Dar	Myanmar	D. Min.	2021
Yee	Meng Chew (Peter)	Malaysia	M.A. Min.	2021
Yoon	Sung (Israel)	Korea	M.A. Min.	2021
Zhang	Chaoyu (Philip)	China	B.A. Min. (Chinese Program)	2021
Zhang	Yingji	China	B.A. Min. (Chinese Program) M.A. Min. (Chinese Program)	2021 2022
Zowa	Munetsi	Zimbabwe	D. Min.	2021
Amilale	Faitala Fio	Samoa	M.A. Min.	2022
Antolin	Joseph Manuel	Philippines	M. Div.	2022
Apineru	Osofua Josie	New Zealand	M.A. Min.	2022
Babilonia	Romeo	Philippines	M.A. Intercultural Studies	2022
Bohnert	Connie Deann	USA	M.A. Intercultural Studies	2022
Burkhart	Paul	USA	M.A. Min.	2022
Cabangangan	Hanah	Philippines	Grad. Cert.	2022
Chen	Yijun	China	M. Div.	2022
Dong	Xile	China	B.A. Min. (Chinese Program)	2022
Kim	Mi Seong	Korea	M. Div.	2022
Liu	Wanzhu	China	M.A. Min.	2022
Loreto	Abdiel	Philippines	Grad. Cert. in Ministerial and Theological Studies	2022

LAST NAME	FIRST NAME	HOME COUNTRY	DEGREE	YEAR GRANTED
Lu	Baole	China	B.A. Min. (Chinese Program) M.A. Min. (Chinese Program)	2022 2023
Ma'u	Samson Moala Lenati	USA	M.A. Min.	2022
Peniata	Fa'amanu Lalotoa	New Zealand	M.A. Min.	2022
Pham	Vu	Vietnam	M. Div.	2022
Ramos	Jazell Robet	Philippines	M. Div.	2022
Sefo	Fata Elise	New Zealand	M.A. Min.	2022
Shitabayashi	Haruka	Japan	M. Div.	2022
Singye	Jimmy	Bhutan	M.A. Min.	2022
Soqa	Daniel	Fiji	M.A. Min.	2022
Tabuya	Jone Duikoro	Fiji	M.A. Min.	2022
Thapa	Sharmistha	India	M.A. Min.	2022
Usero	Milagros	Philippines	Grad. Certificate	2022
Wada	Erisa	Japan	M.A. Min.	2022
Wang	Haochen	China	B.A. Min. (Chinese Program)	2022
Wangyal	Tandin	Bhutan	D. Min.	2022
Yang	Zhouhua	China	B.A. Min. (Chinese Program)	2022
Yoon	Yaesul	Korea	Grad. Cert.	2022
Zhou	Zhen	China	M.A. Min. (Chinese Program)	2022
Zhu	Luwei	China	B.A. Min. (Chinese Program)	2022
Abid	Humaira	Pakistan	M.A. Min.	2023
Benish	Sherry	USA	Grad. Cert.	2023
Borleo	Baby Leen	Philippines	M. Div.	2023
Busocan	Ryan Christian	Philippines	M.A. Min.	2023
Calumpang	Joan Faith	Philippines	M. Div.	2023

LAST NAME	FIRST NAME	HOME COUNTRY	DEGREE	YEAR GRANTED
Chin Jiyh Ping	Ezra	Malaysia	M.A. Intercultural Studies (Islamic Concentration)	2023
Clements	Dianna Michelle	USA	D. Min.	2023
Giesbrecht	Ethel	Canada	M. Div.	2023
Hawley	John Franklin	USA	M.A. Min.	2023
Hsueh	Shannell Debra	USA	M.A. Min.	2023
Kim	Cing Sian Lian	Myanmar	M. Div.	2023
Kok Jin Tick	Albert	Malaysia	M.A. Intercultural Education	2023
Kurniawan	Citra	Indonesia	M.A. Min.	2023
Li	Rui	China	B.A. Min. (Chinese Program) M.A. Min. (Chinese Program)	2023
Loreto	Aesel James	Philippines	Grad. Cert.	2023
Luo	Haitian	China	B.A. Min. (Chinese Program)	2023
Malele-Sivoinavatu	Faith Iliganoa Lialiai	Samoa	M.A. Min.	2023
Malucay	Marc Ceenan	Philippines	M.A. Min.	2023
Manoto	Archie	Philippines	M.A. Intercultural Studies	2023
Mok	Jeannie Frances	Australia	M.A. Min.	2023
Narawa	Emoni Rokomoce	Fiji	M.A. Min.	2023
Pandosen	Gizelle Jaye	Philippines	M.A. Min.	2023
Paraguya	Reynaldo	Philippines	M.A. Min.	2023
Paul	Rachel	Pakistan	M.A. Th.	2023
Peniata	Benjamin Junior	Samoa	M.A. Min.	2023
Pham	Nguyet Thi	Vietnam	M.A. Intercultural Education	2023
Ropio	Aurora Inonencia Javien	Philippines	M.A. Min.	2023
Sangdong	Moses	Myanmar	M.A. Min.	2023
Shibata	Kanae	Japan	M. Div.	2023

LAST NAME	FIRST NAME	HOME COUNTRY	DEGREE	YEAR GRANTED
Soo	Yip Thin	Malaysia	Ph. D.	2023
Taala	Asiasiata Lotofoa Leuelu	Samoa	M.A. Min.	2023
Talingting	Rouselle John	Philippines	M.A. Min.	2023
Tang	Xiaoli	China	B.A. Min. (Chinese Program)	2023
Taoipu	Daniel	Samoa	M.A. Min.	2023
Tran	Lan Anh	Vietnam	M. Div.	2023
Tuialii	Palagikaisa Albert	Samoa	M. Div.	2023
Wang	Jingru	China	B.A. Min. (Chinese Program)	2023
Wu	Guowu	China	M.A. Min. (Chinese Program)	2023
Yang	Ziteng	China	B.A. Min. (Chinese Program)	2023
Yao	Kai	China	B.A. Min. (Chinese Program)	2023
Yohana	Yean	Indonesia	M.A. Min.	2023
Zhang	Zihao	China	B.A. Min. (Chinese Program)	2023
Zhou	Wenliang	China	M. Div.	2023
Zhuge	Huilin	China	M.A. Intercultural Education	2023

APPENDIX B

ASIA PACIFIC THEOLOGICAL SEMINARY
Employees who served APTS for 10 years and above

Current Staff

FAMILY NAME	GIVEN NAME	Starting Date	Yrs	Department
AGLASI	JERSON	September, 2013	10	Housing and Guest Services
JIMENEZ	KRISTINE LEAH	July, 2013	10	Business Office
DUMANSI	ROLLY	March, 2013	10	Housing and Guest Services
RIMANDO	RUVILYN	May, 2011	12	Library
CORPUZ	RODELO	May, 2009	14	Food Services
SACBAT	SOLING	September, 2008	15	Library
CONCEJA	BEVERLY	June, 2007	16	Academic Office
DADO	CHRISTOPHER	September, 2006	17	Grounds
GAPUZ	GRACE CHERYL	May, 2003	20	Business Office
DADO	LINDA	March, 2002	21	Housing and Guest Services
PASCUAL	JOLINA	March, 2002	21	HGS & Academic
MILO	MORENO	October, 2001	22	Maintenance/ Grounds
BALTAZAR	ROMEO	March, 1994	29	Grounds
RAMOS	MERLINA	July, 1991	32	Housing and Guest Services
SEBIANO	ELEANOR	May, 1987	36	Business/ President's Office

Resigned and Retired Staff

FAMILY NAME	GIVEN NAME	Starting Date	Yrs	Department
Ago	Bumanghat	2007-2017	10	Maintenance
Amelia	Dela Pena	2007-2017	10	Housing and Guest Services
Felix	Pacis	2001-2012	10	Maintenance
Carmelita	Vicente	2002-2012	10	Food Services
Wenton	Dolo	2012-2023	11	Maintenance
Albert	Ababulon	2005-2020	15	Maintenance
Bernardino	Baltazar	1992-2007	15	Grounds
Robert	Fanao	1991-2006	15	Maintenance
Tessie	Colar	1986-2002	16	Library
Janet	Apolonio	1990-2007	17	Business Office
Cawaling	Ernesto	1986-2004	18	Grounds
Rudy	Tamayo	1993-2010	18	Maintenance
Mercy	Panelo	2000-2019	19	Dean of Students
Andrada	Benjamin	1987-2007	20	Maintenance
Cheryl Joy	Aquino	1993-2014	21	Business Office
Philip Michael	Aquino	1993-2014	21	Maintenance
Cristina	Fanao	1987-2009	22	Housing and Guest Services
Lucrecia	Gomez	1990-2012	22	President/ Business Offices
Perfecto	Lacuesta	1987-2010	23	Business Office
Sharon	Lapisac	1987-2010	23	Food Services
Araceli	Valdez	1987-2012	25	Housing and Guest Services
Patricia	Escuadra	1991-2017	26	Housing and Guest Services
Joseph	Caluza	1987-2015	28	Maintenance
Royeca	Gloria	1989-2018	29	Business Office

Robert	Ramos	1987-2016	29	Maintenance
Danny	Hill	1987-2016	29	Grounds
Mario	Dela Pena	1992-2022	30	Grounds
Jessie	Dianson	1987-2018	31	Maintenance
Ricky	Caput	1986-2021	35	Maintenance

APPENDIX C

Non-Resident Regular and Part-time Faculty
2004-2023

Name of Faculty	Nationality	Teaching Areas
Aust, John	German	Theology (Systematic Theology I & II)
Davidson, Veronica Doyle	British	Missions
Dooley, Tom	American	Pastoral Counseling
Espiritu, Daniel	Filipino	Homiletics
Howard, Richard	American	New Testament, History, Perspectives in Pentecostalism
Jang, Kwang Jin	Korean	Theology, Pentecostal Missions & Perspective, Pneumatology
Johnson, Alan	American	Missions
Johnson, Melvin	American	Ministry, Counseling, Marriage & Family
Johnson, Sharon	American	Ministry, Counseling, Marriage & Family
LeBret, June	American	Research Methods
McKinney, Evelyn	American	Christian Education, Missions
McKinney, Everett	American	Missions, Leadership
Menzies, Robert	American	New Testament
Oo, Saw Tint Sann	Myanmar	Research Methods, Perspectives in Pentecostalism
Parshall, Phill	American	Hadith and Folk Islam
Phua, Anthony	Singaporean	Biblical Studies, New Testament
Phua, Ruth	Singaporean	Biblical Studies, New Testament
Snider, Kim	American	Intercultural Studies, Education
Sutcliffe, Peter	Australian	Hermeneutics

APPENDIX D

Adjunct Faculty Members Who Have Taught at Least One Course 2004-2023

Last Name	First Name	Title	Course Taught
Albrecht	Dan	Dr.	Pentecostal Spirituality and Ministry- D.Min. course
Arnecillo	Fidel	Dr.	Apologetics
Bagunu	Fel	Dr.	NT Introduction
Bartel	LeRoy	Dr.	Homiletics
Bulkeley	Tim	Dr.	OT Introduction, Wisdom Literature
Bulkeley	Barbara	Dr.	Pastoral Counseling
Chan	Simon	Dr.	Modern Pent. Thought
Chang	Amy		Comparative Religion, Children Ministries, Bib. Theo. & Prac. of Worship
Chen	Joy	Rev.	Discipleship Training, History books (Chinese Program)
Cheong	Simon	Dr.	Homiletics
Chua	Tony	Dr.	World Church History I
Conradie	Peter	Dr.	Curriculum Theory and Dev't
Dalseno	Michael	Dr.	Christian Ethics
Estrada	Nelson	Dr.	Theology of Mark
Gable	Dave	Dr.	NT Relationships- D.Min. course
George	Roji	Dr.	NT Introduction
Gross	Kay	Dr.	Evangelism, Church Management
Hamada	Bahjat	Dr.	Christian Ministry in Islamic Context
Harrison	Jeff	Rev.	OT History
Hernando	Matthews	Dr.	Reformation Theology
Heuser	Roger	Dr.	Managing Conflict & Change- D.Min. course
Huang	Pauline	Dr.	Pers. in World Missions, Pentecostalism, Theo. & Strat. of Miss. (Chinese Program)
Huang	Clement	Dr.	Pastoral Counseling, Systematic Theo. (Chinese Program)
Johnson	Shane	Dr.	Leading the Church in the 21st Century- D.Min. course
Jull	David	Dr.	World Church History I

Kang	Chang Soo	Rev.	Research Methods I
Kao	Shengfu (Paul)	Rev.	OT Intro., NT Intro., Pentateuch (Chinese Program)
Kaufman	Benjamin	Dr.	Leadership in the 21st Century with the Cagles- D.Min. course
Kim	Eun Chul	Dr.	Pers. in Pentecostalism, Exegesis of Acts, Theo. of the Father
Kim	Dong Soo	Dr.	Biblical Foundations for Pentecostal Studies (NT)- Th.M. course
Koenke	John	Dr.	Islamic Course, Ch. Planting Among Resistance Groups
Kowalski	Rosemarie	Dr.	Research Project Seminar, Pentecostal Spirituality and Ministry- D.Min. course
Kowalski	Waldemar	Dr.	Technology in Communication with Rosemarie- D.Min. Course
Lam	Norma	Dr.	Women's Issues in Ministry
Lee	Martha	Dr.	Business as Missions, Spiritual Formation, Intro. to Missions (Chinese Program)
Lee	Edgar	Dr.	Pentecostal Spirituality and Ministry- D.Min. course
Li	Sophia		Church and Missions (Chinese Program)
Lim	David	Dr.	Pentecostal Spirituality and Ministry- D.Min. course
Lim	Stanley	Dr.	Leadership in the Asia Pacific Context- D.Min. course
Lingerfelter	Judith	Dr.	Readings in Pentecostal World Missions with Dr. Judy Cagle- Th.M. course
Liu	Kenneth	Dr.	Systematic Theology II, Theology Since 1500
Long	Gary	Dr.	OT History
Majdali	Kahmeel	Dr.	NT History
Medina	Vince	Dr.	OT Theology
Miller	Greg	Dr.	Reformation Theology
Mittelstadt	Martin	Dr.	Lukan Theology
Moraoka	Takamitsu	Dr.	Advanced Hebrew Grammar
Mour	Joseph	Dr.	Johannine Epistles, Book of Rev. (Chinese Program)
Newberry	Warren	Dr.	History of Missions
Olena	Lois	Dr.	Research Project Seminar- D.Min. course

Pluss	Jean-Daniel	Dr.	Contemporary Pentecostal/Charismatic Issues- D.Min. course
Raman	Suraja	Dr.	Foundations of Leadership & Management
Robinette	Phil	Dr.	Pastoral Care and Counseling- D.Min. course
Ross	Denise		Pers. in World Missions (with supervision)
Rui	Wang Chun	Dr.	The Need and a Proposed Approach for Establishing China Mission Org.
Santonia	Arnold	Dr.	Discipleship Min. in the Church team teach with Dr. Judy Cagle
Scott	Douglas	Dr.	Spirit of God in the OT
Shai	Itzick	Dr.	Intro to Archaeology
Shelton	Lewis	Dr.	NT Intro.
Sorbo	Keith	Dr.	Leadership in the 21st Century Asian Context- D.Min. course
Stossich	Leo	Dr.	Pastoral Counseling
Takatani	Mitsuyo	Rev.	Hebrew I, Hebrew II, Research Methods I (with supervision)
Tan	Joseph	Rev.	OT Introduction
Todd	Stephen	Dr.	World Church History I
Wadholm	Rick, Jr.	Dr.	Former Prophets, OT Intro.
Wang	Bettina		Christian Ethics, Basic Study Method (Chinese Program)
Warrington	Keith	Dr.	Signs and Wonders in Ministry- D.Min. course
Wolfenden	Katie		Church Administration & Finance, Holy Spirit & Min. (Chinese Program)
Wolfenden	Paul		Holy Spirit & Min. (Chinese Program)
Work	Telford	Dr.	Reformation Theology (Chinese Program)
Yabuki	Yoriko	Dr.	Women's Issues in Ministry, Biblical Theo. of Women in Ministry
Yan	Lydia	Rev.	The Book of Romans, Chinese Church His., Life & Teaching of Jesus (Chinese Program)
Yang	Hong	Dr.	Mentoring and Leadership (Chinese Program)
Yang	Esther	Dr.	Found of Leadership & Management (Chinese Program)
Zaprometova	Olga	Dr.	Torah & Pentecostal Spirituality

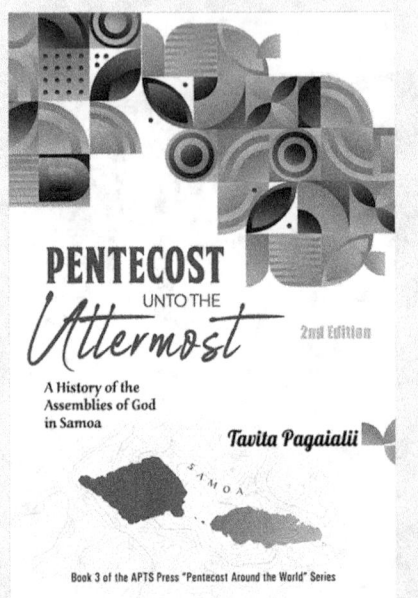

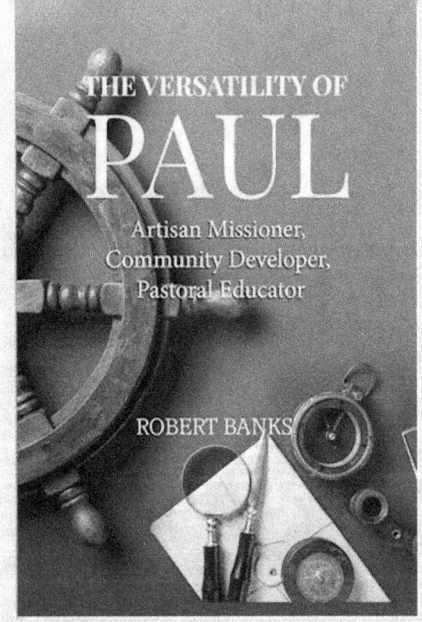

available at www.aptspress.org

available at www.aptspress.org

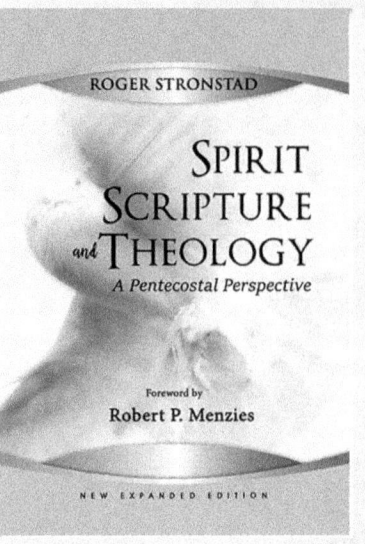

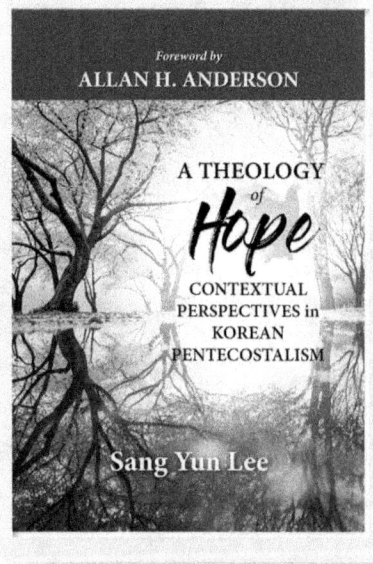

available at www.aptspress.org

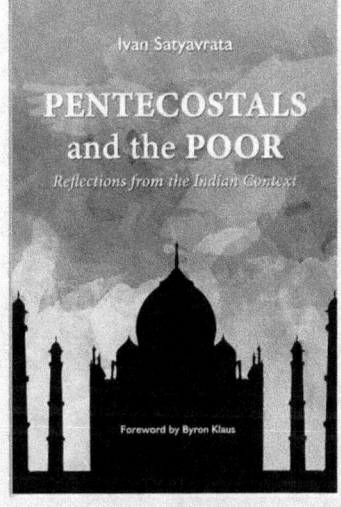

available at www.aptspress.org

available at www.aptspress.org

www.ingramcontent.com/pod-product-compliance
Lightning Source LLC
Chambersburg PA
CBHW051737230426
43670CB00012B/2055